READERS RESPOND TO

No Longer a Slumdog

"I LOVED your book! Recommended it to many others who are also reading it. So eye-opening and inspirational."

—Ms. T.K., Southern Pines, North Carolina

"These children's stories have captured me."

—Mrs. S.N., Gap, Pennsylvania

"These words you put on paper were obviously inspired from our Father. This book brought tears and 'God bumps' to me throughout my reading. Between you, Francis Chan and David Platt, I am so convicted to do more in the name of Christ."

—Mrs. R.H., Lorain, Ohio

"I was truly blessed by the work God is doing in Asia. You have encouraged me to pray for the children and the work."

—Mr. T.L., Tucson, Arizona

"I got your book today and finished reading it within an hour. As a 17 year old with a passion for helping others, this book broke my heart and gave me hope all at once. Thank you for writing such an inspiring book."

—Ms. C.K., Cambridge, Ohio

No Longer a Slumdog

K.P. YOHANNAN

NO LONGER A SLUMDOG

BRINGING HOPE TO CHILDREN IN CRISIS

A DIVISION OF GOSPEL FOR ASIA
WWW.GFA.ORG

Paperback ISBN: 978-1-59589-155-6
ePub ISBN: 978-1-59589-066-5
Mobi ISBN: 978-1-59589-067-2

Published by gfa books, a division of Gospel for Asia
1116 St. Thomas Way, Wills Point, TX 75169 USA
phone: (800) 946-2742

Printed in the United States of America

For information about other materials, visit our website: www.gfa.org

First printing, June 2011   Sixth printing, November 2013
Second printing, July 2011   Seventh printing, April 2014
Third printing, August 2011   Eighth printing, August 2014
Fourth printing, March 2012   Ninth printing, February 2015
Fifth printing, June 2012

With love, I dedicate this book

to the thousands of children

who have found new life and a bright future

through GFA Bridge of Hope.

It brings me so much joy

to see you grow in grace and love.

May your light shine brightly

in the world around you.

TABLE OF CONTENTS

Foreword   11

Acknowledgments   17

Terms and Concepts   19

Introduction   21

1. Stolen Childhood   25

2. Once a Slumdog, Always a Slumdog   41

3. Open Your Eyes   63

4. Winds of Change   81

5. It Is Happening   99

6. What Now?   121

7. Make Your Life Count   135

   Appendix I: Frequently Asked Questions   143

   Appendix II: Believe It or Not   155

   Notes   159

$\mathcal{F}$OREWORD

Before I comment on this book, let me first say a few words about my friend K.P. Yohannan. There are few (maybe no) men I respect more than him. In our day and age, it is hard to find a man who can lead thousands while diverting attention away from himself and onto Jesus. God has graced K.P. Yohannan with this type of humility while he leads millions.

I was able to spend several days with K.P. in India in 2010. It was an honor to spend extended time with one of my heroes. I learned a lot from his wisdom and was surprised by his humor (for some reason, I didn't expect him to be that funny). He is simple—you would never know he is the leader of a massive ministry. His most impressive trait, however, is his love. I left our time absolutely shocked by how loved I felt. You would think that love would flow from all Christian leaders, but sadly, it is a rare trait. I thank God for his friendship and support. The reason why I am endorsing this book and asking you to join in its vision and passion is based on him, the leader of this movement, who follows the Lord and hears His voice.

India is the saddest place I have ever visited. Poverty—coupled with spiritual darkness—makes it one of the most miserable places on earth. These people are stuck in an awful cycle. Smiles are rare, and there is an empty sadness in their eyes. While I have not met the individuals mentioned in this book, I can attest there are many who live under similar conditions.

It is in these conditions that I also have witnessed the transforming work of the Gospel. God is using Gospel for Asia as a light in that world and to millions in more than a dozen nations in Asia, such as Nepal, Myanmar, Bangladesh and so on.

As you read this book, I would encourage you to remember that these are real people we are talking about. They are human beings created in the image of God by a holy God—some of whom you will be hanging out with for all eternity!

In my early days, I would see images on the television of suffering people overseas. I would quickly switch the channel because I did not want to see the suffering. I certainly did not take the time to think of them as individuals with names, lives, families and souls that are just as valuable as my own. I merely labeled them as the "needy" rather than lovely people with personalities. Work hard at seeing their worth. Pray and work for them, as you would want them to do for you if the tables were turned.

I am very thankful for the book you are about to read. It has stirred my heart once again. Living in the West with all of its affluence, it is easy to forget about others. I get focused on my own problems. I forget that one of the best ways to get my mind off myself is by praying for and serving those with greater needs. It is a wonderful opportunity the Lord has given us. We GET to represent Him on this earth by rescuing others as He has rescued us. Few blessings in life compare to the joy we experience when we are used by God to bless those in need.

One of the phrases Jesus used often was "he who has ears, let him hear." His point was that some people change whenever they hear the simple truth. They have "ears to hear." Others will not be affected no matter how clever a message they hear. My guess is that you are reading this book because God has already changed your heart and given you a great love for those in need. Many of us just need to be reminded. Thank you, K.P., for reminding us once again of the amazing privilege we have to represent Christ by serving the poor.

Pastor Francis Chan
Author of *Crazy Love*

Discover More Online

SCAN THIS WITH YOUR PHONE
NoLongeraSlumdog.org

Meet More Children and
See Their Triumphant Stories!

Acknowledgments

Many people have left their mark upon this text and on my heart as they shared their stories with me. I think of Doug Nichols, who pinned me down years ago to be an advocate for the suffering children in this world. I never knew what saying yes would mean. And I am sure this book is in part the fruit of his prayers.

To all the staff who work in our GFA Bridge of Hope centers, I thank you. Without your work and your prayers, these children would never have blossomed, and we never would know what the Lord's hand had done.

Thank you to everyone who has enabled a child to step out of darkness and poverty into the light of Christ. Without your support, these children would still be suffering.

Thank you to my staff who have stood with me during the writing of this book. You have given your lives in labor and intercession reaching all across southern Asia.

Thank you, John—without your impetus, this may never have gotten started.

Kim, thank you for gathering everything together in the beginning and wrapping it all up in the end.

Megan, thank you for your labor of love in working nonstop for months to transcribe, compile and edit this book.

Teresa, my executive secretary, thank you for your unwavering commitment to oversee this project, making sure it was done with the passion I have for these children in crisis.

Thank you, David, for your excellent job in helping to edit this book.

Thank you, Cindy, for the wonderful cover. It has grown on me ever since I saw it.

Special thanks are due to my wife, Gisela, without whose encouragement I would have stumbled many times more than I already have. Your constant companionship and faithfulness have blessed me more than you will ever know.

Most of all, I remain grateful to the Lord Jesus Christ for His constant mercy and grace.

TERMS AND CONCEPTS

ARYAN

The Aryan race, a group of people with fair skin, invaded India from Eurasia more than 3,000 years ago. The name *Aryan* means "royal" or "noble." Because these people believed themselves to be better than the indigenous peoples, the caste system was devised to prevent them from becoming "contaminated" by the darker-skinned natives. Aryans, of course, established themselves as the highest caste.

BRAHMIN

Brahmins comprise the highest caste of the Hindu religion. Although they only make up approximately 5 percent of the total population, they hold the lion's share of the power in India's political, educational and corporate spheres.[1]

CASTE / CASTE SYSTEM

According to Hinduism, people have an intrinsic value and are sorted into different groups called "castes." This insidious system that has served to segregate the population and turn people against each other is based purely on their genetics.

DALIT / UNTOUCHABLE

The word *Dalit* literally means "broken," "crushed" or "oppressed." In Hindu society, Dalits are at the lowest rung of the ladder. The vast majority of them are impoverished, exploited and powerless to change their fate. Considered to be polluted or unclean, they are called "Untouchables." If they were to touch someone of higher caste, the upper-caste person would supposedly become contaminated. This is why many Dalits are not allowed to drink from community wells and are discouraged from attending schools with other students.

GFA BRIDGE OF HOPE

GFA Bridge of Hope is the children's outreach ministry of Gospel for Asia International. This ministry brings the prospect of a brighter future to Asia's poorest children through education, physical assistance and the Good News of Jesus. Our desire is to minister to at least 500,000 children in the near future.

HINDU

Hinduism is the main religion in India and is the basis for the continued existence of the caste system.

OTHER BACKWARD CASTES (OBCs)

The term *OBC* applies to those from the lowest castes, also known as Sudras. The OBCs are higher than Dalits but are still oppressed and impoverished. Sudras are thought of as the slave caste.

SLUM

With great numbers of people moving to cities in hope of a better life, the population inevitably grows faster than what the government can sustain. The result is millions of people living in destitute conditions. "Slum" is the name given to the areas where such poor people dwell. These people have no homes, no land, no plumbing or infrastructure and often no education. Most slums are filled with Dalits and OBCs.

TRIBAL

The tribals are the original people of India. Today they are still found throughout the country, often in the jungles, mountains and forests of the land. Like the Dalits, tribal people are exploited by the upper-castes.

INTRODUCTION

Have you seen the award-winning movie *Slumdog Million-aire?*[1] If you haven't yet, you should. I can't think of anything that has made me sad like certain scenes in this movie have.

In the film, you see the harvesting of street children by a deceitful, greedy pimp. His bottom line is to get them to beg and collect money for him. He even turns some into sex slaves!

One of the most gruesome parts of the movie is when a 7- or 8-year-old boy is blinded by this cruel man. The pimp actually poured boiling oil into the boy's eyes. A few years later he is seen, still begging, standing in a dark tunnel off a busy street in Bombay. For those caught in begging rings, there is always this fear of being mutilated by a boss in order to gain more sympathy with passersby. Kids who have been disfigured can bring in more money for their pimp. Although this treatment is the exception, there are nonetheless millions of children trapped in a life of begging. I wish these scenes were only fiction in a movie, but unfortunately, what is depicted is reality for countless youngsters.

Each beggar child has some sad story as to how he or she ended up on the streets of Bombay, Delhi, Calcutta . . . and there they are exploited by those who find them.

In India alone, there are 50 million children who work from age 4 on.[2] They labor from morning until night for pennies, often making only 10–15 cents per day. The majority are Dalits or from one of the Other Backward Castes (OBCs).

These children live in enormous crisis, and I assure you that their suffering causes great pain in the heart of the Living God. At the same time, they present us with a tremendous opportunity to bring hope into their worlds through the love of Christ. They are a part of the 4/14 Window, the 1.2 billion children on this planet between the ages of 4 and 14.[3] As followers of Christ, we are told by our Lord not to neglect, not to ignore, not to forget these precious, helpless children.

Gospel for Asia has missionaries and social workers who serve among the 1 million dwellers in the Daravi slum in Bombay[4] where the movie *Slumdog Millionaire* was shot. Gospel for Asia is reaching out to needy children like these all across South Asia. To date, in Christ's name we have been able to rescue 72,000 children from a life of bondage (as of 2014). Each one is enrolled in a GFA Bridge of Hope center. But what is that compared to the millions of children trapped in a life of hopeless wandering on the streets?

My heart's cry is, "Lord, enable us to rescue at least 500,000 children from despair and hopelessness. Please help us be a part of rescuing these boys and girls from a future of being blinded, maimed, disfigured or forced into the life of a street beggar."

I am sure your heart, like mine, can feel the pain of these precious children. Together we can make a difference, and we will. We must.

Thank you for joining me on this journey to learn more about these precious little ones who are desperately crying out for hope.

Sometime in your life, hope that you might see one

starved man, the look on his face when the bread finally

arrives. Hope that you might have baked it or bought

or even kneaded it yourself. For that look on his face,

for your meeting his eyes across a piece of bread, you

might be willing to lose a lot, or suffer a lot,

or die a little, even.

Daniel Berrigan[1]

CHAPTER ONE

STOLEN CHILDHOOD

Muttu was born in a small hut in a slum near Madras. His parents died when he was barely 7 years old. His uncle took Muttu and his younger sister to live with him. Unfortunately, this man was an alcoholic and a drug addict and would often both starve and abuse Muttu and his sister.

One day the two children were taken to the neighboring state of Kerala and sold to Rajan, a beggar mafia pimp. Here they became part of a group of beggar children involving at least 10 others about their age. They were told to beg on the streets and return all the money they collected to Rajan. Muttu became afraid when the other children warned him that he would be severely beaten if he didn't bring back enough money.

Every night Rajan came, often drunk, and took what money the kids had collected that day. On one occasion Muttu did not earn enough to please Rajan. Rajan became irate and beat the helpless lad. In the end, Muttu was dragged to a distant place where Rajan continued to punish him. As Muttu cried out, the angry pimp forcefully closed the young boy's mouth. Then Rajan took a can of kerosene and poured it over Muttu. He set the child's body on fire and left him to die.

Fortunately, someone found him, lying unconscious and covered with rags, and took him to the hospital. More than 50 percent of his body was covered with burns. Even after Muttu regained consciousness, he was unable to say a word for several weeks. For months he suffered excruciating pain.

Muttu did eventually recover, but he still lives in a state of fear. He says the worst part of the whole experience is the agony of not knowing what happened to his little sister.

This story first appeared in India's national newspaper *The Hindu* under the title "A Lonely Battle for Life."

We cannot even begin to imagine something like this being thrust onto a child. It is harsh, it is cruel, and it never should happen. But the sad reality is that it did occur.

When I hear stories like this, I think back on my own life growing up, reflecting on the many blessings and hardships that I faced. It helps me see things from a different perspective.

Let me ask you, what was your childhood like? Your parents probably started planning for you even before your conception. Your medical care began while you were still in your mother's womb. In all likelihood, your mother gave birth to you in a sterile hospital room, surrounded by well-trained doctors and nurses.

After a clean and safe delivery, you probably were taken home to a wallpapered nursery and brand-new baby blankets. You were fed on demand and kept warm, clean and protected from harm. To prevent any serious illnesses, you received all the required immunizations. As you grew into a healthy child, you were given clean clothes to wear and toys to play with.

When you reached school age, your parents took you to the store to buy your school supplies. If you were like most children, your mom sent you off to school in bright new clothes with a nourishing lunch. Maybe she even drove you there herself.

Does this treatment of children sound strange or unusual? Not at all. It is completely normal in countries and homes of financial means. Even acknowledging that there are unfortunate exceptions, I doubt anyone reading this book would disagree that this kind of security, provision and education are a child's birthright.

A Far Different Reality

The reality for children born in developing countries is often a far cry from what I just described. The tragedy for untold millions of children living today is that they have never had even *one* of these childhood experiences. Imagine if this was you:

Your parents saw your conception as both a blessing and a curse. They knew that in a few years there would be more hands to work, but also that you would put even more strain on the meager food supply. Prenatal care for you was lacking because there were no medical facilities in the remote village or slum where you were born and your parents could not afford to travel away from home to find one.

After a risky home delivery on the dirt floor of the family shack, you were dried off with a dirty rag or an old newspaper; your parents never learned much about sanitation.

Your home was made of tarpaulin sheets held up by bamboo sticks. It was pretty crowded with your whole family living in less than 100 square feet of space. The shack was right next to a railroad track, and every 10 minutes a train would come roaring through. Sleep was difficult under these conditions.

When you were born, you were already malnourished. The little milk your mother was able to give you couldn't do much to

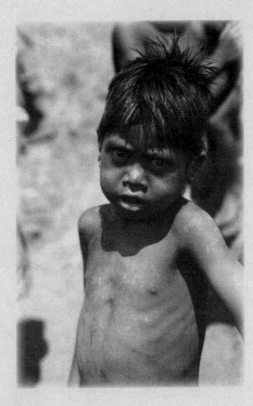

Many children throughout the world live in a perpetual state of hunger and pain, their bodies struggling to keep up with the demands that are placed on them.

ensure your growth. You might also suffer night-blindness from vitamin A deficiency.

Soon your mom had to resume her day job of cleaning streets with a hand-broom and washing other people's clothes, because when she didn't work, the family didn't eat. So you were left in the care of an older sibling. As you started to crawl, you explored on your hands and knees the open sewer trenches running along the alley between neighboring shacks. If you had any clothing at all, it was made from rags found in the nearby dump, which is where all the household treasures came from.

If through strength and providence you survived the first few years of life, at the age of 5 or 6 you might be sold by your parents into bonded labor to help secure a little desperately needed money for the family. Otherwise, you probably joined your siblings sifting through garbage to find rags, plastic bottles, pieces of metal or anything else that could be sold for a few pennies to help the family survive. You may have become a beggar or even a thief, desperately doing whatever you could just to eat.

School? It wasn't even a possibility. Your small contribution to the family income was needed just to survive. Besides, nobody in the family had ever been to school anyway.

You think I'm exaggerating. No, I am not. According to UNICEF, more than *1 billion children* around the world are deprived of one or more of these essentials: adequate shelter, food, safe water, sanitation, health care or education—living in conditions you and I can hardly imagine.[2]

See what it takes to be a first-generation reader.

▶ Third-Grade Dropouts
www.nolongeraslumdog.org

DESPERATE POVERTY

As bad as this sounds, millions of children every year experience a far worse fate. In despair of ever being able to care for you, your mother might one day have thrust you onto a passing train bound for Delhi, Bombay or Calcutta. At the end of the run, you would have been pushed onto the streets of a megacity by a train employee as you screamed in vain for your mommy. It is hard to imagine this could really happen—but it does. I heard this very story told by a girl named Asha. Here's her tale in her own words:

My name is Asha. Six months ago, my sister Lata and I got on a train with our mom. She told us we were going to Bombay. We were excited because all the movies in India are made in Bombay! We love watching movies, and we always wanted to ride a train.

Lata and I pushed through the other passengers and squeezed into our seats with our mother. We had a lot of fun looking out the windows at all the trees and fields passing by. The train made stop after stop at junctions along the way. I did not know when we would get there, but I thought it must be soon because we had traveled so far. At one of the stops, Mom stood up and said to us, "You girls stay here. I'm going to get something to drink." But after a few minutes, the train started moving again, and Mom still wasn't back!

We were so scared that we didn't know what to do! We held our hands together and stayed as close as we could. Our hearts were racing. The train left the junction and kept going faster and faster. Hours passed. Where was Mom? No one seemed to know or care.

After many hours, the train finally stopped at a big, loud station. I was in tears. I decided that we should get off. There were people everywhere, pushing and shoving. Lata and I stayed close together, but we did not know where to go. I thought that maybe someone could help us, but I was too scared to talk to anyone! We sat together in a corner, waiting for *something to happen. I don't know what. We waited for several hours.*

As the sun started to set, a kind-looking woman came and asked us what was wrong. We told her that we had lost our mother. She led us to a shelter where we could stay, a place for other girls who were lost or didn't have their families.

It feels like it has been a long time since that day. Our mother still has not found us, but I am glad we are at the shelter. I don't know what would have happened to us if we had stayed at the station.

Due to acute poverty in the rural villages, abandoning children is a choice that some parents are almost forced to make. An online search reveals even more about the horrible situations in which children in this generation find themselves trapped.

In India alone, there are 11 million children like Asha who have been abandoned, and 90 percent of them are girls.[3] Three million of these children end up living on the streets.[4]

We encountered one such street child just outside one of our GFA Bridge of Hope centers; she had been living on the railroad tracks. At about three in the afternoon, as all the students were going home, one of the staff members saw a little girl standing all alone with her head down, weeping and not saying a word. She couldn't have been more than 9 years old.

The teacher approached her to ask what was wrong, but she could not stop crying. Eventually, in barely a whisper, these words came out: "My brother also died."

Then her story started to tumble out. Her parents had died several years earlier, and she had been left living on the railroad tracks with her brother. That was until he, too, recently passed away.

The little girl said that the children she used to play with were all gone. They left her and were now in our center. So she had come to ask, "Would you take me too?"

Due to the acute poverty throughout southern Asia, almost half of the children there live without adequate shelter. Some have homes made of whatever materials they can find, while others simply sleep on the streets.

Of course we did. But the sad reality remains that most such children do not find a place of hope like this.

Throughout the slums of southern Asia, there are millions of children living with only one of their parents. Many dads and moms have died because of easily preventable diseases. Some are simply overworked, their bodies failing because of exhaustion and undernourishment. If the father is gone, it becomes even harder for a family to survive. There is a huge social stigma attached to being a widow that makes it very difficult for the mom to get a job.

Even when both parents are alive, they spend so much time working menial jobs just to survive, like cleaning streets or working in a landlord's field, that they end up with few hours to spend at home with their kids. Children left in such conditions easily become rowdy and uncontrollable.

This is just what happened to two young boys living in a slum in Andhra Pradesh. Their father had left the family in order to go to Bombay, where he thought he could make some money. Vichy and Tusli, ages 9 and 7, quickly became quite disobedient.

The father had thoughtfully left their mother some money to help care for the family while he was gone, a sum of Rs. 1,500 (US$33.00). Vichy and Tusli promptly stole it and wasted it.

Their lives were spinning out of control. They would wander around the slum stealing from people, harassing other children and generally being troublemakers. Everyone considered these boys a headache, but no one knew what to do with them. Many were actually afraid of them and didn't want to stir up any trouble for themselves.

When Yadav, the leader of the local GFA Bridge of Hope center, found out about the plight of this family, he was burdened by the Lord to help. He made arrangements for these two brothers to be enrolled in the center. It took a great deal of patience just to get these unruly boys to sit through their lessons. Yadav devoted a lot of his time to helping them and would pray

Without an education, impoverished children have almost no chance of ever escaping the hardship in which they are trapped.

for them as he taught them how to live. Slowly he instilled discipline into them and demonstrated respect and kindness while sharing lessons from the Bible.

The two boys started to change, and eventually, their lives turned around completely. Now Vichy, the older one, likes to visit the same people he used to harass and share the love of Christ with them. Instead of calling him "headache," now the people in the slum call him "Little Pastor."

God is able to work amazing transformations in the lives of such children, and we have seen Him using GFA Bridge of Hope to bring hope into their lives. But for the millions of children still waiting in the rural villages and slums, there remains little chance of change unless we get to them soon.

Calcutta alone is home to more than 100,000 street children[5] who know neither father nor mother, love nor care. They are left to fend for themselves, resorting to whatever means necessary just to survive.

One of the most shocking reports I ever read appeared in the *Indian Express* several years ago. On the front page was a photo of a little boy, half naked, lying on the sidewalk of a busy street. Next to the boy was a dog. Upon closer inspection, I saw that it was a female dog, and the little boy was actually sucking her milk. The caption read, "This Dog Is His Mother." The three-column article went on to describe the heartbreaking agony that homeless children face as they try to survive on their own.

That article came out several years ago, and I wish I could report that things have gotten better. But I can't because the media keep telling me otherwise.

During one of our weekly prayer meetings, a staff member presented a story he had read recently on the BBC News website.[6] Here was a photo of two little children from North India, maybe 3 or 4 years old. Their stomachs were distended eight to ten inches out from their bodies. They lived near a quarry where their parents worked. The earnings from their backbreaking hours of labor produced enough for only one meal a day. In their desperate hunger, the children had eaten mud from the quarry, making them sick. In fact, one of the two was already showing signs of early kidney failure.

It breaks my heart to see such suffering, especially knowing this has been going on much longer than I have been alive.

CRUEL EXPLOITATION

Children in underdeveloped countries are often the victims of cruel exploitation of various kinds. Throughout the world, more than 150 million children between the ages of 4 and 14 are involved in child labor.[7] There are 1.2 million children bought and sold every year.[8] Those who end up on the streets are quickly picked up, like the boys in the movie *Slumdog Millionaire,* and forced into a begging ring or other hard labor. Child laborers of South Asia toil to make fireworks, twist carpet fibers or make matches in primitive factories. They spend their days in quarries and coal mines, rice fields, tea plantations and pastures.

One girl labored in the fields of a cottonseed farm in southern India, earning 20 cents an hour. This 15-year-old was continually exposed to the highly toxic pesticides that were sprayed on the fields every week, where she has been working since she was 10. She started working when her father committed suicide after incurring huge debts.[9]

An article in *Forbes* magazine tells of six to eight young boys crammed together in a room no bigger than a king-size bed. They work 16 hours a day, decorating photo frames, diaries, shoe heels and such with sequins and pieces of glass. Some are as young as 5 years old. They all live together in this same room and cook their food together. Their combined earnings each month might be US$76,[10] which means each child only makes US$9.50 each month!

The worst fate of all awaits little girls who end up trapped in prostitution. Some are kidnapped or tricked into it. Parents sometimes sell their girls, similar to the way children are sold into bonded labor. Others are dedicated to this life as a sort of offering by their parents. The book *Dalit Freedom* brings this practice to light.

Thousands of untouchable female children (between six and eight years old) are forced to become maidens of God (Devadasis, Jogins, a Hindu religious practice in Andhra Pradesh, Karnataka, Maharashtra, and Orissa, to mention only a few). They are taken from their families, never to see them again. They are later raped by the temple priest and finally auctioned secretly into prostitution and ultimately die.[11]

Other girls, and some boys, are simply caught on the streets or kidnapped from their homes. There are more than1.2 million children involved in prostitution throughout the Indian subcontinent; many of them are from Nepal or Bangladesh.[12] Children's Care International explains:

Recruiting children for the purposes of prostitution is done in the same way as for child labourers: they are bought and sold. Many children, however, are simply kidnapped. . . . The little girls find themselves locked up in brothels or end up in national and international prostitution networks. The children must first reimburse the money given to their parents plus the interest—an astronomical amount that becomes an eternal debt. They are forced to remain sexual slaves because of this debt, which is impossible to reimburse because it increases daily. . . . The majority of these children suffer from serious physical and psychological problems, and their life expectancy is about 15 years.[13]

Millions of children are trapped in bonded labor, sold into prostitution or abandoned every year.

My heart aches as I hear what is happening to God's innocent creations. It is hard to realize this is not a novel, this is not a movie, and this is not even a nightmare. This is reality—reality for millions of children on the earth at this very hour.

The reason for such brutality, pain, abuse and all suffering is, in a word, sin. This sort of agony is not the way God meant for us to live when He created us. But Satan came to destroy, tear down and kill (see John 10:10), and he is at the source of this heartache, leaving these children hurting and destitute.

Looking into their faces, you won't see innocence and trust, but rather hunger, pain, suspicion and fear.

When we see their plight, we ask ourselves, why is this happening? Is there an answer to their suffering? Who are these desperate children in crisis, and what can we do to bring them hope?

"You hear, O LORD, the desire of the afflicted; you encourage them, and you listen to their cry, defending the fatherless and the oppressed, in order that man, who is of the earth, may terrify no more" (Psalm 10:17–18).

The biggest disease today is not leprosy or tuberculosis, but rather the feeling of being unwanted.

Mother Teresa[1]

CHAPTER TWO

Once a Slumdog, Always a Slumdog

Bihar, the poorest state in Northwest India, is known for its deprivation and misery. The majority of the population is made up of desperately poor Dalits, tribals and Other Backward Castes (OBCs).

A few years ago, a story appeared in a national newspaper that revealed once again the plight of these desperate, suffering people. The story was shocking; a young and destitute mother sold her newborn for 10 pounds of rice!

I could hardly believe what I was reading. A picture was included of this fragile yet truly beautiful girl, maybe in her mid-20s, with tears running down her face. She was crying as she told the reporter, "I want my baby back."

When she was asked, "Why would you sell your baby for 10 pounds of rice?" her answer was even more disturbing. She replied, "What do we do? People like us are starving to death . . . at least my baby will live. I will die anyway, like many others here. Even the 10 pounds of rice will not save me."

Poverty, grief and hopelessness were etched on her face and the faces of those who flocked around her.

WHO ARE THESE PEOPLE?

These are the Dalits and the Other Backward Castes.

They have had to break their malnourished bodies, working all hours of the day simply to get enough money for one meal. Why? It is more than just poverty, though they are among the poorest in the world. It is more than just their lack of education, though only 30 percent of them can read at all.[2] It is because of the caste system and the fact that they are not a part of it.

This oppressive way of life for the world's most impoverished all began with the arrival of the Aryans in India, about 1500 B.C. Because the Aryans believed themselves to be a superior race, they devised a cruel system to prevent themselves from becoming "contaminated" by the indigenous peoples. This system also served to help control the populace, making them view each other through a distorted lens of inequality.

Through this tactic, the Aryans were quickly able to become a rich and highly educated minority. Instead of using physical weapons, they used this mind-bending tool called the caste system. This system taught that people were reborn from different parts of the body of their god Brahma and thus had differing value.

Thousands of years later, people still believe that those who came from the head, arms and shoulders of Brahma are intrinsically better than those who came from the torso, legs or feet. This is the premise and justification used to abuse those of lower caste.

The caste system also divided society based on roles or jobs. The four main castes, from the greatest to the least, are *Brahmins* (priests and teachers), *Kshatriyas* (rulers and soldiers), *Vaisyas* (merchants and traders) and *Sudras* (laborers and servants). Within these four main castes, there are countless subcastes that further divide and categorize the Hindu population.

Caste is determined at birth. If, for example, your parents were of high caste, you would also be of that caste. However, if your parents were low caste, that's where you would belong. You would grow up learning to fear and respect those who are higher and despise those who are lower.

There is no opportunity for advancement, no hope of someday being worth more. Whatever you are, you always will be.

The caste system, though officially outlawed in India, is still a major source of social identity and ostracism. It is because of their caste that many of these children suffer.

Your caste not only affects your sense of worth, but also the jobs you can hold, what clothes you can wear, where you can worship, who you can marry, where you can gather water and what sort of education you can expect.

This pervasive system of social ostracism and prejudice is the glue that keeps everyone in their proper place, even in modern India where caste-based discrimination is officially prohibited by law.

The Bottom of the Bottom

At the very bottom of the system, below all four castes and all the subcastes, is a group of people called "Untouchables" or "Dalits." The word *Dalit* means "oppressed" or "broken." They are considered by other castes to be subhuman, impure from birth and worthy of nothing but contempt. To be "Untouchable" means just that—no upper-caste can touch you, and you cannot touch them either. Anything you contact is declared unclean. If anyone were to stoop low enough to give you something to eat or drink, be assured that it will be in a cheap disposable dish. Further, it is expected that *you* will throw away what you just "contaminated."

Often Dalits are denied access to public wells for the same fear of contamination. In an article published October 25, 2010, I read of three Dalit men who were fined Rs. 15,000 each (US$330) because they drank from a public water fountain used by the upper-castes.[3]

The majority of these exploited peoples live in rural villages and communities, slaving away to eke out a living. But there are also millions of Dalits and OBCs who try to live crammed into the slums. Those on the outside looking into the slums began to see these people in the same way they saw the wild animals that run down the narrow dirt streets. This is where the name "slumdog" comes from.

I cannot fully imagine what it would be like to be a Dalit, even though I have seen and read so much. The following poem helps shed light on what it must be like. It is written from the perspective of one of their children.

> I am nobody
> Worthless my life is
> To Untouchables I was born.
> A Dalit child my fate sealed.
>
> I was born in slums
> Rights? We have none
> To upper-caste our lives we owe
> Slaves to serve all their wish.
>
> Poverty and hunger
> Is all I ever knew
> If there is hope
> Tell me how?
>
> What is my future?
> Do I have any?
> It all looks so dark
> And I wish I was not born.[4]

For 3,000 years, hundreds of millions of Untouchables have suffered slavery and oppression at the hands of their fellow countrymen. Many truly believe they have earned this life and have no right to expect anything different.

Heart-Wrenching Decisions

Often the Dalits are driven to extreme measures just to make ends meet. I don't know how they can stand making these heart-wrenching decisions, such as giving away an 8-year-old son or daughter to be a bonded laborer for an upper-caste landlord or selling their body as a prostitute. Then they must live with the mental anguish of making such choices.

I recently heard of a young woman who had to make such a decision. In the year 2000, Geeta was married at the young age of 17. She had her first daughter just a year later in 2001. Shortly after their marriage, her husband lost his job, got involved in illegal activities and became an alcoholic. In early 2003, he left Geeta while she was pregnant with their second child, a son.

Totally alone, Geeta started going from house to house, washing dishes to make a little money. She would also make floral garlands to sell, but it was never enough. There was no one to help her, and she faced her difficult life alone.

Because they lived in the slums, she felt that her children's character was being ruined and their future looked dim. They were often starving or half-fed. Rent was difficult to pay, and education for her children was all but impossible. Geeta hoped her situation would improve, but it only got worse. She eventually became so desperate that she seriously considered selling her half-starved body into prostitution.

It was at this critical juncture in 2006 that Gospel for Asia started a GFA Bridge of Hope center in the slum where Geeta lives. Both her children were enrolled, and they were finally getting not only an education and food to eat, but also

See life through Geeta's eyes.
New Hope for a Slum Widow
www.nolongeraslumdog.org

a stable and safe place to grow. They began to blossom under the teachings of Christ.

Geeta was counseled by our staff workers, and they often prayed with her. God in His mercy gave her a laborer's job in a factory. And now that her children are sheltered by our GFA Bridge of Hope center, they have a bright future too.

I praise God that He rescued Geeta from the agony of having to make such a terrible decision. There are still many, however, who have few options for employment. They will do whatever they can just to make enough to eat.

INTENSE LABOR

The filthiest, most degrading and menial work in society is relegated to Dalits. They are the ones who harvest the fields by hand, working for hours in backbreaking labor. They are the ones who clean the open-air toilets, latrines and sewer lines with their bare hands.

I remember hearing the sorrow of a little boy in a GFA Bridge of Hope center who lost his mother. She performed backbreaking labor, toiling all day long. She would go into the nearby forest to collect dead wood. Then she would carry it on her head to the nearby market to sell as firewood. All of this was just to earn a few rupees, an amount that was never quite enough to feed their aching, empty stomachs. I remember feeling his hurt and wrote this poem at the time:

Hear more about "The Stick Gatherer."
The Stick Gatherer
www.nolongeraslumdog.org

Dark, skinny body—this was my mother
Eyes sunken with pain
Turns and looks at us
As she disappears into the woods.

It is late in the afternoon
We children had eaten nothing all day
Waiting and watching for mother
After selling the sticks to come home with food.

Our father left for a neighboring state
Looking for a coolie's job
For Untouchables here like us
There is no job except cleaning latrines.

Poverty and hunger took its toll
My mother died without help
My brothers and I did not know what to do
Wandering on streets all day long.

Our father came home a broken man
Held us in his arms crying bitterly
He sits and gazes into the dark
Mutters to himself I don't know what.

The sun rose with bright hope
Some kind people took us to school
At first I didn't know much at all
Now I know we have hope.

Often my eyes seek my mother
I still cry and grieve
When I see a dark skinny vendor of wood,
I wish I had money to buy her sticks.[5]

And we all wish there was some way we could help.

I am so glad that this boy was able to find hope in the midst of his grief. But the sad truth is that all too many have yet to hear of this God of hope and are breaking under the burden they carry, thinking that only a life of hurt awaits them.

Excluded from the caste system, "Untouchables" do all the tasks that others consider "unclean," including disposing of corpses, cleaning up human waste and performing other labor-intensive jobs. Like the woman in the poem, people can often be seen carrying large loads that strain their fragile bodies.

DEVOID OF RIGHTS

Those at the bottom are routinely denied even the most basic human rights. Violence is rampant. Degradation against Dalits is so pervasive that the Indian legislature passed something called the "Prevention of Atrocities Act," spelling out the illegality of such things as parading people naked through the streets, forcing them to eat feces or burning down their houses. Nevertheless, thousands of acts of public humiliation and group violence, such as lynching and gang rape, continue to take place. It seems that the rules of untouchability don't apply to acts of violence or sexual abuse against Dalits.

A Dalit might be beaten to death just for asking for his daily wages. On June 16, 2009, an article by *Thaindian News* reported that a 48-year-old Dalit laborer had been attacked by a group of men in Uttar Pradesh after asking he be paid his salary that had already been withheld for an entire month. Five men in total attacked and killed the Dalit worker by beating him mercilessly with wooden sticks.[6]

For the most part, Dalits have no one to turn to for help. Because they are at the bottom rung of the proverbial social ladder, they have little chance of ever getting their case through the courts.

Crimes against Dalits are rarely reported to authorities because of the fear of reprisal. Sadly, the police will often turn a blind eye even when they know the full story.

I remember hearing of a Dalit girl who was raped by several men. Her parents were told by the girl's attackers not to go to the police, but they did anyway. A few days later, they found the dead body of their daughter lying in a field.

It is nearly impossible for us to imagine the mental anguish Dalits live with, growing up as children in a society that views them as expendable, being called worthless and treated with contempt. We must hurry to reach those who continue to live in pain and darkness. Worse than all the abuse, than all the discrimination, the backbreaking labor and constant hunger are the feelings of hopelessness they experience every day.

STUCK IN THE CYCLE

All too many Dalits get trapped in bonded labor, a kind of indentured servant arrangement in which poor families can pay what they owe through work. In hopes of clearing debts faster, it is not only the parents who are involved, but their children as well. Often the whole family will work for the lender, usually someone who is in an upper caste.

Some families were sold into servitude when the parents were still children and never escaped it. The debt to a landowner or employer may be small, but the interest rate charged often exceeds what they are paid. The result then is that they can never repay what they owe. This is especially true when these poor people are illiterate, as they often are. Because they cannot read or write, they are incapable of keeping records of the work they have done, the amount they owe or the amount they have repaid.

But beyond being trapped in debt and bonded labor, their mindset is also ensnared.

The conditioning works something like this: you can tie a dog to a stake, and it will run in a circle. After a long time, you can actually remove the stake and the dog will still run in the same circle. It no longer thinks of going into the field because it is so accustomed to the limitations of the rope. It accepts that it cannot go any further, so it stops trying.

Likewise, Dalits have lived their entire lives thinking there is

Millions are trapped by their caste, stuck in the mindset that things cannot change and will not change.

nothing better for them, that there is no hope of change or freedom. For them, it does feel that their fate truly is "once a slumdog, always a slumdog."

Niran John Das grew up living in this as reality, until one day everything changed.

> *I was born and brought up in a Dalit society where we were very much oppressed and downtrodden by the higher people. There are a lot of people who practice untouchability here, who won't share a bench with someone from a low caste or share food with them or anything.*
>
> *I went to school up to third grade, but I had to*

discontinue when my father became ill. Suddenly there was no one to support the family, so I, being the eldest son, had to start working. My dreams were all shattered. I worked in house construction, making and carrying bricks or cultivating the barley and wheat fields.

We didn't have breakfast, and we didn't have lunch; all that we had was dinner. I was so hurt and very sad when I saw that we worked hard the whole day but only made enough for one meal while others who didn't work as hard had more than enough. We were sometimes paid late, and then there was no food at home.

Sometimes we would take a debt to pay for our rent, and then we would have to take more. You know, it is kind of a cycle. You get debt and you work. You are not able to pay back and so you keep working for them. And that's what used to happen to us.

Even when my father became well enough to work, we still could not afford school for any of us. Our family and our needs had grown. He went to the neighboring state to look for a job and took me with him.

While we were there, he came to know the Lord Jesus and became the first believer in our village. My father used to pray and read the Bible and take me to church. But I was not interested at that time and went back to my home village.

Later I was married, and we both were working for the landlords. I always wondered, When are we going to improve this situation? I have to get liberated from all this kind of bondage.

And it is a bondage. But the problem was, even though I wanted to get freedom from this, I could not because we were not educated. I didn't understand how to get liberated. I wanted freedom, but there was no way to get out. In the society that I grew up in, it is destined. I could not become a higher-caste person because the cycle is always there, and this is what I believed. It was all normal life for us.

After some years, I became sick and could not tell east from west, and I could hardly stand. My family did all sorts of pujas and rituals for my healing, but nothing worked. My father came, and for six years he prayed for my healing, shared the Gospel with me and encouraged me. But then one night, he asked some other Christians he knew to pray for my healing. My family who did not know the Lord said, "If Jesus can heal him, then we will accept Jesus as our Savior." That was the challenge they set.

As my father prayed, I felt a strange kind of feeling. The next morning, I was able to ride my bike again. I was completely healed. The whole village was shocked. They had not known Christ could do such a thing.

Because of this miracle, I gave my life to the Lord. I understood that I was freed from the bondages of the caste system. In Christ, there is no high caste and no low caste. And when the barrier is not there, I'm no longer under bondage. I'm free only in Christ.

And this is what I love. My main desire is to go and make people here in the village realize that we can be freed. If people can realize there is no difference in a person, whether from a Dalit society or from high society, their bondage will be broken. Their eyes

will be opened. So I always pray, every day, that the
people in my village should realize we are all the
same in Christ.

I praise God that the cycle of oppressive thinking Niran
John Das had lived with all his life was finally broken through
the all-surpassing love of Christ. This man has been completely transformed. From a life of thinking he was worthless and
destined to perpetual servitude,
he has now embraced his dignity
and freedom in Christ. I pray there
will be many more who experience
this miracle—hundreds of thousands more!

Find out more of what God is doing
through Niran John Das now.
Three Minutes in a Dalit Village
www.nolongeraslumdog.org

A SCOURGE IN OUR TIMES

Most of the unfortunate children who beg on the streets of
South Asia's cities, labor in its fields and factories or die a thousand deaths as child prostitutes are Dalits. They are the most
disenfranchised of the disenfranchised, the least of the least, the
little ones who have no power to change their world. So they remain as they are, trapped in the slums and the fields of Asia.

In India today, there are about *250 million* Dalits. That means
almost 20 percent of India's population is considered subhuman
and treated like dogs.[7] Seventy percent of Dalits live below the poverty line, and at most 3 percent of Dalit women can read and write.[8]

Slightly above Dalits on the caste ladder is another huge group of people, an estimated 500 million more.[9] They belong to the Other Backward Castes. They also suffer abuse and injustice at the hands of the upper-caste minority. The two groups combined represent a population that is well over twice that of the United States. In fact, more than one out of every 10 people alive on planet earth today is either a Dalit or an OBC.

Can you think of any system in history that has so adversely affected such a large percentage of the world's population as this scourge of the caste system has? I can't.

These masses of people grow up without hearing about the love of Jesus. They live without peace, suspecting there is something fundamentally wrong but not knowing how to change things. These are the "harassed and helpless" Jesus talked about (Matthew 9:36).

One woman among these masses is Indrani. She grew up in a Dalit Gypsy family, traveling from place to place. Her parents taught her how to drink when she was a girl, and also how to smoke, gamble and beg. She thought her ways were normal. Later she lived in a small hut the government granted to her clan. She made maybe Rs. 50 per day (US$1.10) through her begging, and her husband made about Rs. 100 per day (US$2.20) working on fences. They had eight children, all of them girls.

Indrani did not want her girls to be raised the same way she was but didn't know how she could make a difference in their lives. Thankfully, Indrani met a missionary named Joseph, who told her about GFA Bridge of Hope. Her girls were soon enrolled.

They learned about Christ, hygiene, discipline and manners, reading, respect and general self-control. But their learning didn't stop with them. The girls took these lessons home.

Indrani marveled at how they were maturing, wishing that she had such an opportunity when she was young. But then she thought, *If my children are able to change, why can't I?* So she started to pray to the Lord and go to church. She gave up her drinking, her gambling and her tobacco use. Now the whole family prays together every day. They have all become a part of a local congregation and are growing in the Lord.

Learn about Aruni, Indrani's daughter. Eight Sisters Change Family Legacy www.nolongeraslumdog.org

Our work to rescue the suffering does not end with just one child's bright future and newfound hope in Christ, but hope is carried on to their family, relatives and community.

Although the caste in which they were born dictated that this family would never be able to change, they were completely transformed. I hate to think about what the life of Indrani's eight girls would be like if they too grew up believing they were only good enough to be slumdogs and beg for a living.

HOPE AT LAST

God has always been in the business of redemption—just think of the Israelites. He saw their affliction. He heard their cries. He knew their sufferings. And so He came down to deliver them. This is the story we read in the book of Exodus when some 600,000 Israelites were finally freed after 400 years of captivity.

Likewise, God has seen the 250 million people who have been living in perpetual servitude for the past 3,000 years. He knows the plight of the 50 million child laborers in India.[10]

We know that God's ears are attentive to the pleas of the captives. Jesus said He came for this very purpose: "The Spirit of the Lord is upon me, because he hath anointed me to preach the gospel to the poor; he hath sent me to heal the brokenhearted, to preach deliverance to the captives, and recovering of sight to the blind, to set at liberty them that are bruised" (Luke 4:18, KJV).

God the Almighty was moved with compassion over the suffering, oppression and slavery of His people, the "children of Israel." It might be interesting to note that the Dalits are also called "Harijan." Although it has now become a derogatory term, it is a name that literally means "children of god." God cares about the suffering of the Dalits as much as He cared about those who were slaves in Egypt.

And how did He respond?

When God saw their suffering, He told Moses, "I have indeed seen the misery of my people in Egypt. I have heard them crying out because of their slave drivers, and I am concerned about their suffering. So I have come down to rescue them from the hand of the Egyptians and to bring them up out of that land into a good and spacious land, a land flowing with milk and honey. . . . I have seen the way the Egyptians are oppressing them. So now, go. *I am sending you*" (Exodus 3:7–10, emphasis mine).

When God spoke to Moses, naturally we might assume that God Himself was coming down to earth to do this rescuing, saving work. Right?

No.

Instead, God says to Moses, "Go. I am sending *you*" (Exodus 3:10, emphasis mine).

If God were coming down to save His people, why did He

send Moses? Not because He *needed* Moses' strength and arm of the flesh, but because He chose to work through him, just like God still *works through us* to carry out His will. This is important to recognize. Although God is fully capable of accomplishing all He desires on His own, He still uses us in His incredible work.

God used Moses to guide Israel out of Egypt and to tell the people how to be saved from death through the Passover Lamb. The night after they took shelter under the blood of the lamb, they were led out of their slavery.

Countless millions of Dalit villagers and slum dwellers, including their children, all need to be set free from the bondage of sin and slavery. They have yet to hear of the Lamb that was slain from the foundations of the earth (see Revelation 13:8). And they will only hear of Him when you and I, just as Moses did, obey the call of God.

We know the cries of these little children ascend day and night to heaven and that God knows their suffering. There is nothing on earth God is not aware of.

Our hearts ache to change their worlds and make things right. We pray that they too might have life and have it more abundantly. Yet how much more does God Himself yearn for His own creation? He knows all these children personally.

He is the One who said, "It would be better . . . if a millstone were hung around his neck and he were thrown into the sea, than that he would cause one of these little ones to stumble" (Luke 17:2, NASB).

The question is, when *we* hear the cry of the suffering children and the Dalits, can we obey the voice of God and be part of the answer?

I believe we can.

"I want to lift them up. When I go to villages, even different places, I see people who are without food even. I groan within me. And I think, 'How can I help them come out of all this poverty and oppression and this kind of problem?' That's my burden."

—Niran John Das, missionary from India

You can give without loving, but you cannot love without giving.

Amy Carmichael[1]

CHAPTER THREE

OPEN YOUR EYES

Long ago there lived a very rich man. He was so wealthy he could buy anything he wanted. His palace, beautifully adorned with all sorts of luxury items, was the largest building for miles. He was able to eat whatever his heart desired. His clothes were stylish and clean, and he had numerous servants. In all his life, he never knew a day of want.

On the street in front of his mansion lived a poor beggar. The only clothes he had were the ones on his back, and they were tattered. His hair was long and scraggly, and he was quite sick. His body was covered with sores, so terrible and oozing that the street dogs came and licked them. Every day he would sit in front of the gates of the rich man's estate, begging for scraps of food. Then one day the poor beggar died, and angels carried him to God's paradise.

In time, the rich man also died. He went directly to hell. He is there to this day, crying out in desperation for just one drop of water to cool his tongue. The response he gets is always the same: "You enjoyed your luxurious life on earth without one thought about the helpless, defenseless beggar who sat by your gates. Now see what has happened. You will suffer in hell and Lazarus, the man you neglected, is in paradise with God. He will live in absolute delight forever, and nothing can take this from him.

Likewise, nothing can change this terrible fate of yours; it is sealed" (see Luke 16:19–25).

Obviously, I have paraphrased the story Jesus told in Luke 16. Please don't misunderstand; the rich man did not go to hell simply because he was rich. If we look through the Bible, there are many people like Abraham, Joseph and David who were all exceedingly rich, even ruling kingdoms and dynasties, and they were completely devoted to God. Their riches did not lead them to their eternal destination. Likewise, it was not poverty that sent Lazarus to heaven.

The reality is, it is not the physical or the obvious externals that become the reason why one goes to heaven, but rather a relationship with God manifested in choices made. The rich man's uncaring attitude toward the poor and suffering revealed his life apart from God. If he knew God in reality and walked with Him, he would have cared for Lazarus. It is plain throughout the Bible that God doesn't want us to ignore the poor, the defenseless, the hungry or the hurting.

Look at Acts 10, where we read the story of a Gentile named Cornelius, a devout man who feared God. Two additional things are written about him. He prayed continually and *gave alms generously to the people.* The inward heart of Cornelius, the devout, God-fearing part, was displayed outwardly in his generosity. God sent His great apostle Peter specifically to meet with this Gentile and share the Gospel with him.

God is sad when He sees His people living selfishly, only concerned about "me and mine." It especially hurts Him whenever Christians close their eyes to the pressing needs before them.

Are we like the rich man? My prayer is that we will all take

FREE BOOK REPLACEMENT COUPON

Please send me another copy of *No Longer a Slumdog*.

Please circle: Mr. Mrs. Miss Rev.

Name _____

Address _____

City _____ State _____ Zip _____

Phone ( ) _____

Email _____

☐ I give Gospel for Asia permission to send me emails (i.e. field stories, urgent prayer requests, etc.).
☐ I give Gospel for Asia permission to send me text messages (i.e. urgent updates. etc.).
Privacy Policy: Gospel for Asia will not sell, lease or trade your personal information.

I gave my copy to:

Please circle: Mr. Mrs. Miss Rev.

Name _____

Address _____

City _____ State _____ Zip _____

Phone ( ) _____

Email _____

HB52-PB9C

GOSPEL FOR ASIA

> Give this copy of *NO LONGER A SLUMDOG* to a friend, your pastor or anyone else you think would like it.

> Mail this completed card to us and we'll send you another copy of the book absolutely free!

Sharing the book is a great way to help change the lives of children in South Asia.

PASS IT ON!

If you want to pass this book on to someone else, **we'll give you a new one!**

Your stamp on this card is like an
additional donation!—Bro. K.P.

fold before tearing

Sponsor a child, get news
from the mission field
and order other
GFA materials
online at

WWW.GFA.ORG

this warning seriously. How many more cars, clothes, toys and trinkets do we really need before we wake up and realize that half the world goes to bed every night with empty stomachs and naked bodies?

Turn through the pages of this book. Look at the faces of these beautiful children God is weeping over. The Lord is looking for those who will share His heart. Open your eyes and look at the reality that is before you.

Remember what Jesus said, "Whatever you did for one of the least of these brothers of mine, *you did for me*" (Matthew 25:40, emphasis mine). This means that whatever we do for the least of these, whether good or bad, it is as though we have done it for Christ Himself. In other words, the beggar Lazarus sitting neglected in front of the rich man's gate was, in reality, God lying there.

When we hear about the millions of suffering, hurting children in the world, let us not look the other way. Each one represents our Lord Himself.

JESUS CARES

Over and over in Scripture, we recognize God's heart for those who have no voice, for the captives and the oppressed. There is a divine passion for them, a heavenly desire for their well-being, because God prizes them highly and His heart breaks to see them suffer.

The Scripture is crystal-clear about God's heart for children. The best place to look is at Jesus, because He is the exact representation of the Father's nature (see Hebrews 1:3). Jesus Himself says, "Anyone who has seen me has seen the Father" (John 14:9). Therefore, we can be sure the fullness of God's heart for children was perfectly reflected in the life and words of His Son. So what can we learn from Him?

Throughout the Gospels, we see Jesus repeatedly speaking about how important children are to Him and to the Father. In Mark 10, we encounter Jesus surrounded by people, teaching them the truths of God. Some of the parents in the crowd started bringing their children to Him so He could bless them. The disciples rebuked these people and started practicing crowd control. They may have said something like, "The Master is teaching an important message. Please sit down and keep your children quiet."

Jesus would sit and give children His undivided attention, and He commands us to do the same in His name.

This passage states that when Jesus saw what was happening, He was displeased and told His disciples, "Let the little children come to Me, and do not forbid them; for of such is the kingdom of God" (Mark 10:14, NKJV). He actually interrupted His teaching, put His hands on them and blessed them. In the midst of His busy ministry, Jesus stopped everything He was doing to show these children His love and interest.

Watch Ashok's joy as he experiences his heavenly Father's love.
Ashok and His Heavenly Father
www.nolongeraslumdog.org

In Mark 9:37 (NKJV), Jesus said, "Whoever receives one of these little children in My name receives Me." What does His statement mean to us?

Imagine that you have worked all day and are finally sitting down to dinner with your family. Suddenly, you hear a knock on the door. You aren't expecting anyone, so you look through the peephole thinking you will maybe see a salesman or someone who wants to mow your lawn. Instead, you see the King of the universe.

You would break down your front door to welcome Him in!

But what if you see a starving child, half-naked, with more holes than cloth in the rags she is wearing? Her hair is unkempt and filled with lice; her face is covered with dirt and sweat. Would you break down your door to welcome her in?

Jesus tells us that anyone who embraces little children, who loves them and who gives them dignity and value in *His name* is actually doing these same things for Jesus Himself (see Matthew 18:5). But there's more to it than that. Jesus is so happy with anyone who cares for children in His name, that He will come and be with them in a special way. He tells us further in

Mark 9:37 that we receive not only the Son, but God the Father also. So there is a special blessing for those who share the heart of the Eternal for His children.

Do Not Despise Them

In Matthew 18:10 (NASB), Jesus said, "See that you do not despise one of these little ones, for I say to you that their angels in heaven continually see the face of My Father who is in heaven." According to the dictionary, the meaning of the word *despise* is "to regard as unworthy of one's interest or concern."

Jesus is warning us that when we hear about needy children, we need to be careful not to see their plight as unworthy of our attention. We can't simply say, "Yes, I know it's awful. Those terrible people hurting children should be stopped, and the little ones should be loved and cared for. But there's nothing I can do about it."

Do you think Jesus cares about children who live on the streets? Do you believe He sees the boys and girls laboring long hours in the fields and firecracker factories? Does He identify with the pain of devastated young girls caught in the degrading life of prostitution?

He sees. He cares. He feels their pain.

Now He has given us the opportunity to see them too. The question He is asking is, How will we respond? Will we look away and steel our hearts against their pain?

I must confess that in the early years of the ministry, I was blind to these kids. Although I had been confronted by them all my life, my heart didn't break for these desperate children like

Jesus said, "Let the little children come to me, and do not hinder them" (Matthew 19:14).

it should. Then one day the Lord got my attention while I was standing at a busy street corner in India waiting for the light to turn green.

There were little children everywhere, a common sight at many busy corners in Bombay. Tourists are cautioned not to give them anything because once you do, the others will all mob you.

While I was at this corner, feeling a bit annoyed by little hands grabbing at me, I heard from behind me the voice of a young girl.

"Sahib, Sir, my father died. My mother is sick. She can't beg anymore. And I have a little brother, who is very hungry. Would you please give me a few pennies so I can buy some bread and take it to him?"

The light turned green, and everybody hurried on. But I couldn't move. What she said pierced my heart. I turned around and saw this young girl, not yet 10 years old. I will never forget her face—one of the most beautiful faces I have ever seen on a child. She had big brown eyes, thick black hair almost the length of her body, dirty fingernails, and dust mingled with sweat running down her face. She was barefoot and in rags. She just stood there with her hand extended.

I put my hands in my pocket and took out all the money I could find and gave it to her. Then I walked on.

Like the disciples on the road to Emmaus, I felt like an unseen stranger joined me on this emotional walk. The silent question He asked was deep and penetrating, "So what do you think about the little beggar girl you just met? Is her life as valuable and precious as . . ." and the face of another young girl appeared in my mind's eye. I didn't know the name of the girl on the street, but I for certain knew the name of this new face; it was my own little daughter, Sarah.

The two were approximately the same age, but their lives could not have been more contrasting. Sarah had her own carpeted room with furniture and toys and every comfort one could imagine. My wife, her German mother, made sure she was well taken care of. Her sheets and pillowcases were changed every week on her comfortable bed. She had plenty of clothes, socks, tennis shoes, a toothbrush, toothpaste, soap and shampoo. We had given Sarah all of what is so abundantly available for children born and raised in the United States.

But for the Indian street girl I had just encountered, I doubt that she had ever held a toothbrush in her hand. Her face had never been washed with soapy water, and her hair had never been touched by shampoo. She had never slept in a warm bed under clean sheets and on fluffy pillows. Maybe she had never even heard the words, "Your mommy loves you. Your daddy loves you."

Probably her entire upbringing had been one of daily struggles—living on the streets with thousands of other children who also had no home to go to when evening came.

This question just kind of hung in the air as I walked on, "Is her life as valuable and precious as . . ."

I knew what the proper response was. Being a minister and quite familiar with the Bible, I knew right away what my answer was *supposed* to be.

"Of course, Lord! I care about her. The value of this little beggar girl's life means as much as that of my own daughter's."

No more questions were asked. I was left to process my own thoughts. What followed was one of the most difficult walks of my life. It was the first time I realized the pain and passion our Lord carries in His heart for the forgotten children in the villages and slums of these poor and destitute nations.

Honestly, I had great trouble trying to assimilate this revelation. I couldn't imagine my daughter standing on that street in Bombay with her hand out begging for a few pennies to buy a piece of bread for her brother. It was too painful for me to think about.

Yet the reality remains that the girl I met represented the faces of millions of children who are crying out not only for food, but also for help and love and hope . . . yet they can't find any.

I certainly don't want anyone to feel guilty about lovingly caring for our own children and grandchildren. But the question remains: Is there also room in our hearts for one or two of the world's millions of suffering children, and can we also care for them in Jesus' name? Can we see them as Jesus does, so special to Him, their worth like jewels beyond compare?

Are we willing to have our hearts break with His at such sights, knowing there are children who suffer so much in this life *and* have no hope of heaven in the next, simply because they know nothing of the hope that is in Christ?

I believe, as followers of Christ, we are commanded to reach out to the least of these in the name of Jesus and show them they matter a great deal to God, who sacrificed His only Son to reach them with His love.

We must learn to look away from our own worlds to care for what God cares about. Let's not devote our energies into trinkets and mindless self-indulgence that have no eternal value, but instead learn to invest in these children God cares about so much. They truly are the least of the least—the ignored, unfed, abused and unloved. And we are told by our Lord that we cannot turn a blind eye to their plight.

SPECIAL ASSIGNMENT

Our Father in heaven is greatly concerned about the welfare of these helpless children. In fact, God has special angels assigned to watch over them at all times. Let us look again at Matthew 18:10 (NASB): "See that you do not despise one of these little

Every time a child is saved from destruction, the angels in heaven rejoice with the Father.

ones, for I say to you that *their angels* in heaven continually see the face of My Father who is in heaven" (emphasis mine).

Now this is something very significant that Jesus is telling us here. There are angels watching over each little child in the slums of Bombay, yet simultaneously, these angels are looking into the face of the Father who is sitting on the throne.

How happy these angels must be when someone feeds these little children, values them, teaches them, prays for them and loves them!

This is what happened to a young lad named Nadish.

There were people who cared for him and prayed for him, and I'm sure the angels were delighted to see him set free.

This is his story.

My mother enrolled me in a Bridge of Hope center, but I was not very interested in my studies. I preferred to play and go out at night.

One day my mother said to me, "Nadish, you need to pay attention to your studies!" This made me angry.

I went out that afternoon to buy some medicine for my mother. I was still unhappy and did not want to go home, so I wandered around for a little while. I got lost near the rail station. The sun went down, and I began to get scared. I didn't recognize this place.

A nice-looking older man came by and saw that I was lost, so he offered to let me stay with him for the night.

I wish I had not gone with him.

He took me to a place far away, and before I realized what was happening, he sold me to a landlord.

The landlord forced me to clean up animal manure all day, and when I was done, he would lock me in a small room with the animals. I soon learned to ignore the smell.

Days turned into weeks, and my stomach would continually growl. He never gave me enough to eat.

Weeks turned into months, and my body would ache. The work was hard, and there was never enough time to rest.

Months turned into years, and I began to think that this would never end. I was trapped, alone, locked in this dark place with the other animals.

Then one day something strange happened.

There was another boy. He had been captured too.

He cried a lot. He, too, was hungry. He, too, never got enough rest. But it was nice to have someone to talk to. He told me about his family and how he had gotten captured. I told him about my mother. I missed her very much. I had no siblings, and my father was dead.

I told him about the Bridge of Hope center. There were people there who loved me, and there was always a meal.

We worked together at the stalls. Because there were two of us, the work was easier—not because there was any less, for our taskmaster always found more work for us, but simply because there was someone to talk to. For several months, we went on like this.

Then one night, something amazing happened. The landlord forgot to lock the door! We could hardly believe our eyes. We snuck out that night and ran as fast as our tired legs could carry us.

We made it to the police station and told them what happened. They arrested that man and freed five other boys.

I was then reunited with my mother. She cried a lot when she saw me, always saying, "I was hoping some day you would be back."

I asked her if I could go back to the Bridge of Hope center. I'll be starting back very soon.

It feels so nice to wear a clean pair of clothes! To eat a full meal! To take a bath and be washed! I can smile and laugh again.

I still am scared of the dark, and I don't like to go

out at night. I keep thinking this is all a dream, that one day I will wake up in that room again, but so far that has not happened.

I found out that the people at the Bridge of Hope center were praying for me. They had been for two years.

I do not know, but maybe that is why the man forgot to lock the door.

How happy the angels in heaven must have been to see Nadish free and behold his joy in the face of the Father!

Throughout Matthew and the other Gospels, we see how Jesus repeatedly highlights how important children are to Him. His heart is very close to them. He wants us to know that "when you embrace My children, you embrace Me. To touch them is to touch Me."

A Heart Like His

If you are a parent, you understand this sentiment. Who doesn't take it extremely personally when someone treats their child with special kindness? On the flip side, what parent wouldn't experience an explosive fury to learn that their child had been abused?

Close your eyes and just imagine it was *your* child who was gagged and bound and whose eyes were blinded by boiling oil. Picture *your* daughter trapped in a cage with lines of men outside. If your heart doesn't start pounding with an adrenaline rush, there is something wrong with you.

Our Lord's whole life is summarized in His mission statement, "I came to seek and save that which was lost" (see Luke 19:10). He gave Himself completely for others. Matthew 8–9 covers a period of His intense, nonstop ministry. After days of pouring Himself tirelessly into people who were suffering emotional pain, physical sickness and demon possession, the writer Matthew relates that Jesus was "moved with compassion" for the people He was seeing (see Matthew 9:36, NKJV). To Jesus, the people looked like sheep without a shepherd—hurting and lost with no one to care for them.

Matthew wrote his Gospel 30 years after the event. What do you think he must have seen in Jesus' expressions that would have been so memorable that he would record this impression so many years later?

Quite possibly, Jesus had been acting like someone who just learned of the death of a son, daughter, husband or mother. He may have been completely overcome by emotion, weeping, and He may have even lost his appetite. Maybe His legs crumbled under Him so that He could hardly stand.

Why do we picture Jesus as a stoic? Surely when He saw His own creation—the work of His hands, the people He made in His own image—being destroyed and abused, it grieved Him deeply. His heart must have felt like it was about to break. And Matthew records 30 years later: "We saw it."

It seems, though, that Jesus mourned alone. Matthew doesn't say, "We were moved by compassion too." Maybe the disciples' hearts were hard and could not feel the pain of the suffering multitude.

Although these children are rejected and despised by their society, God sees them the same way He sees us: precious beyond compare.

Jesus closed up His earthly ministry with the words, "As the Father has sent me, I am sending you" (John 20:21). We are sent into the world to show His love, but we cannot show His love until we have His heart.

God is grieved over the plight of children in this generation—children who, this very moment, are suffering in circumstances we don't even want to imagine. He is looking for individuals who will say no to themselves and instead care for the things on His heart, individuals who will tell these kids that Jesus loves them and will embrace them in His name.

Like me, I am sure that when you hear about the suffering of these downtrodden children, their parents and their families, you want to change their circumstances. You want to comfort them in their pain.

I feel sad about those early days when I didn't see these lost children the same way I saw my own. I was blinded by my own agenda, so busy in the ministry that I couldn't see the face of Christ in theirs. But then God in His mercy helped me identify with His heart for those who have no voice.

And now my prayer, like many before me, is that the Lord would break my heart with the things that break His.

"I realized that God loves me, and I also have started to love me. I thank God who has brought me so far."

—Talan, GFA Bridge of Hope student

*T*he first question that the priest . . . and the Levite asked
was: "If I stop to help this man, what will happen to me?"
But the Good Samaritan . . . reversed the question:
"If I do not stop to help this man, what will happen
to him?"

Martin Luther King, Jr.[1]

CHAPTER FOUR

WINDS OF CHANGE

"Give me liberty, or give me death!" is the famous proclamation by the American patriot Patrick Henry. This is the heart's cry of every human being. And who among the free would desire that others should suffer oppression, abuse or hurt?

We ache inside when we hear about the awful suffering of starving children at refugee camps and in disaster zones. It troubles us when we read about Adolf Hitler's concentration camps. We can't forget the images of thousands of helpless people—mothers, fathers, old and young—all crammed together behind electric fences. Their bodies are skin and bones, their eyes sunken with despair. Worse than seeing the pictures is knowing that many of these victims were forced into gas chambers. It makes us both angry and terribly sad.

In his book *Roots,* Alex Haley describes the plight of African people who were packed into slave ships, sent to America and sold like animals in the market. This was despicable. We ask ourselves, "How could human beings do such things to their fellow man?"

Look at the French Revolution and how the people got fed up with tyranny. In 1789, they set about to stop it. And the oppression that occurred in Romania is a more recent example of a population that suffered tremendous abuse until they wouldn't stand for it any longer. As generations had done before, they too worked for liberation. These shifts in social order are all proof that no matter how powerful a government or system becomes, people will not put up with such ill treatment forever.

In each of these cases, there came a time when someone said, "Enough!" A revolution started—some violent, others more peaceful—and soon had the support of all those with eyes open to see the plight of the suffering masses. Few people simply stood by and watched once they realized there was something they could do to help.

God steps in to save those who are suffering. To free the children of Israel from the slavery they had been under, He subjected their Egyptian slave masters to awful punishments, culminating in the death of every firstborn in that powerful empire.

The worst, most pervasive form of slavery that exists in our time is the caste system under which millions of Dalits and OBCs suffer. No other people alive today have been mistreated for as long as they have. Now they are finally saying, "Enough is enough! We will not put up with this anymore."

Hope on the Horizon

Today, after endless years of bondage, winds of change are blowing on the Indian subcontinent. In the late 1990s, a grassroots Dalit human rights movement started to challenge the dictates of caste segregation. This movement birthed the hope of freedom in the hearts of many Dalits and OBCs. Leaders emerged from this massive group of 750 million people to seek out justice.

These new Dalit leaders realized that the only way for them to escape the oppression they were under was to quit the Hindu religion and its caste system. They sought to embrace faiths that gave them dignity and value and brought hope to their children. They wanted a religion that saw all human beings as equals.

The turning point came on November 4, 2001. On that day, tens of thousands of Dalits gathered in Delhi for a history-making meeting in which they publicly declared their desire to "quit Hinduism" and follow faiths of their own choosing. I was humbled to be invited to speak as one of the few representatives of the Church. The night spent in anticipation prior to the rally is one I will never forget.

The streets were packed, though thousands were prevented from coming because of the upper-caste opposition. These people stopped

Many Dalit leaders recognize that in order to break the bonds of caste, children will need more than just a good education; they will have to embrace a religion that views all humans as equals.

many Dalits from entering into Delhi for the freedom rally. Despite this, tens of thousands of people were able to attend, and each one was eagerly looking for hope. I was excited to be a part of it.

I remember my words as I stood before these masses who had been exploited for so long: "My precious brothers and sisters, I come to you today speaking on behalf of Christ, His love and His mercy for us all. Jesus came to set the captives free. He Himself said that 'whoever the Son sets free is free indeed.' . . . We love you with Christ's love, unconditionally and always."

Watch footage from November 4, 2001.
2001 Dalit Gathering in Delhi
www.nolongeraslumdog.org/dalits

This is what Jesus offers when He says, "I have come that they may have life" (John 10:10).

To grasp their logic in declaring a desire to quit Hinduism, it's important to understand the Hindu-based belief in karma and reincarnation. That is, how a person lived their previous life determined the outcome of this one, including the caste into which he or she was born. For someone to be born as a Dalit, below the feet of the Hindu god Brahma, basically means they were terrible in their previous life and this is their time to suffer the consequences.

This explains the shame and ill treatment heaped upon them; many Dalits genuinely believe abuse is their proper due. But if one should renounce their belief in reincarnation, the chains of fatalism will be broken.

That is what has happened in the hearts of millions of Dalits in the past decade. In spite of a violent backlash against their liberation, I believe a corner has been turned and major change is inevitable.

Gospel for Asia was eager to reach out to the Dalits during this time of enormous transition. The greatest need among these poorest peoples of southern Asia, their leaders declared, was for their children to become educated. Simply knowing how to read would go a long way to protect them from being cheated in written contracts. It would open doors to better jobs with higher pay. This would allow them to finally get out of debt, which would end the cycle of bonded labor.

Unfortunately, the reality is not so simple. Centuries of oppression, nationwide poverty and the constant teachings of inequality are not so easy to overcome. We understood that a good education alone would not be enough to bring immediate economic and emotional healing. As I mentioned in my first book, "The only weapon that will ever effectively win the war against disease, hunger, injustice and poverty in Asia is the Gospel of Jesus Christ."[2]

They need education, and they need the truth. And when they know the truth, they shall be set free (see John 8:32).

Massive Obstacles

India's National Policy in Education, written in 1986, aims at making free primary education available to all children, including Dalits. For many reasons, however, they rarely attend school. The main problem is poverty. Many of these families simply cannot survive without the income their children make. If they were to go to school during the day, there would be no food for them to come home to. Bonded-labor contracts effectively kill any chance for education. Also, government schools are often too far away for the children to reach by foot.

The truth is that free education isn't really free anyway. There are fees, plus books and school supplies that are needed. Proper clothing is expected too. All of these requirements cost too much

Although education is supposed to be free, many parents can't even afford the supplies their children need in order to attend school.

for most poor families. According to one of our social workers who ministers to slum children, most of them have only a single change of clothes. He says, "When we tell them to bathe and change their dress, they can't. So they will go home and wash, but the next day they will come in the same dress."

In addition, Dalit children who try to attend school usually find it a painful experience. Biases against Dalits and OBCs are often present in the classroom. They may be required to do tasks, like cleaning the grounds, which other children don't have to do.

There are still communities in which Dalits are not allowed to attend the same schools where upper-caste children study. And even where Dalits are allowed in, they will typically have to sit in the back of the classroom and not participate in class activities. They are often verbally abused and are more likely than other children to receive corporal punishment. Teachers have been known to say that Dalit pupils cannot learn unless they are beaten.[3]

If a low-caste pupil has trouble learning a school subject, they don't have anyone at home to help them. Most parents were not allowed to go to school when they were young, so they themselves cannot read or write. All of these factors work together to discourage a student from persevering in their studies.

These are formidable obstacles to overcome, both economically and socially. Gospel for Asia stepped out in faith to bring education within the reach of these children in crisis. We didn't realize at the time how great an impact this would have on everyone involved.

ENCOURAGING BEGINNINGS

One of our early attempts at running a school program was among the Banjara tribe. The tribal leader personally asked me to help educate their children. We were learning as we went, but the Lord was faithful, and those first efforts were wildly successful.

Reports soon came in about the impact of these efforts in these tribal villages.

Students were captivated by the love of Christ they heard about and received in tangible form from their teachers. They went home and talked about what they were learning, and their parents started getting excited too. Soon new congregations sprang up in the region.

These changes did not escape the notice of nearby communities. Before long, leaders in those villages pleaded with our mission leaders in charge to start schools for their children too.

THE DREAM

The school program was starting to grow, but I confess that I struggled with how people might respond to our new initiative. You see, my mission has always been to preach the Gospel, establish local bodies and disciple those who come to know the Lord. Whereas others in the Body of Christ might be called to minister aid and comfort in this life, I knew that the eternal destiny of people was infinitely more important.

I don't want to suggest that I am hard-hearted and have no concern for human suffering. Since its beginning, Gospel for Asia–supported missionaries have been agents of compassion and were among the first to help victims of catastrophes like the Orissa cyclone in 1999.

As Christians, I believe we must do all we can to alleviate pain and suffering in those around us. This sort of concern for others is a natural fruit of the Gospel. But we must never minister to someone's physical needs at the expense of preaching Christ.

The Great Commission that Jesus gave literally means we share the Gospel of grace that the Lord Jesus Christ came, died and rose again to bring us salvation. This is fundamentally important. This is why the idea of expanding this new initiative, one that seemed more centered on social justice and compassion, was difficult for me.

So before we expanded this program further, I, along with my senior leaders, sought the Lord for confirmation that this was the direction He wanted us to go. We entered into a time of intense prayer and fasting. Soon, I had a dream that God used to propel us forward.

I was standing in front of a vast wheat field looking out upon a harvest that was clearly ripe. I stood there for a while overwhelmed at the sheer size of the harvest. What seemed like endless acres continued for as far as my eyes could see.

Watching the golden wheat sway in the breeze, I got this sudden understanding that I was looking upon the fields that Jesus spoke about in John 4 and Matthew 9. It was as though the Lord was telling me this harvest was free for the taking, much like Psalm 2 tells us to ask for the nations and He will give them to us.

Overcome with excitement at seeing such a great harvest ready for reaping and knowing this represented millions of souls being rescued from an eternity in hell, I began to jump up and down with excitement.

I could see it. The harvest was plentiful. It's ready! And I was so happy. I ran toward this field shouting, "Wow! We can take it! All these people we can take to heaven!"

As I raced toward the field with all my might, I was already thinking about printing tracts and missionaries going door-to-door to tell people about the Gospel proclaiming the Good News to everyone in sight! This is what I knew of bringing in a harvest.

But I was wrong.

I suddenly couldn't go any farther. Right in front of me was a river so wide and raging that I dared not step closer or try to cross it. I had not seen it from where I was standing before.

I just stood there in agony, thinking, *Oh my goodness. The monsoon will come soon. It's all going to be destroyed. What am I supposed to do?*

My heart broke. Was I only going to look at the harvest but not be able to embrace it? I stood there weeping, feeling so helpless and full of despair.

All of a sudden there appeared before me a bridge reaching from one side of the vast river to the other. It was not a narrow bridge, but one that was very broad. It was completely filled with little children from all over Asia—poor, destitute children, like those I'd so often seen on the streets of Calcutta, Kathmandu and other Asian cities.

Then it was as though someone spoke to me and said, "If you want to have this harvest, it's all yours. But this is the bridge you must cross to get to it."

I woke from my dream and realized the Lord was speaking to me about something incredibly significant: If we follow His instructions, we will see millions find hope. And our ministry to the children will be the bridge to help them experience the love of Christ.

I shared this dream with my colleagues, and together we

The Lord showed us that if we can reach out to these poor and marginalized children in His name, they will act as a bridge to reach their parents, their communities and their people.

concluded that God had given us a call to bring hope to the children of Asia. Through this "bridge of hope," children would be given an education and, at the same time, be taught about the Lord. They would experience His love, and their families and communities would also hear that Jesus loves them. The opportunity was overwhelming. But knowing the Lord was behind it was all the wind that we needed.

Hope in Crisis

By providing quality education to the poorest of the poor, we enable them to rise above the oppression they have lived in for centuries. And the positive response from the downtrodden is often overwhelming. Not only are the lives of children completely transformed by the simple love of Christ, but their families also are being touched and finding hope.

From my experience, I have seen that the message a child hears growing up can affect them all through their lives, whether they are encouraged to succeed or told they are worthless. My trust in the Lord began when I was a small child. My wife was the same way. The knowledge that He loved us stabilized our lives and prepared us to face the future. I am sure you can recognize in your own life how the things you learned when you were young affected the way you saw yourself and the world as you grew up.

The book of Proverbs teaches us that if you instruct a child in the way he should go, he will not depart from it when he is old (see Proverbs 22:6). If we bring these children the message of God's love for them, teaching them that they have great value in His eyes and are not limited by the caste into which they were born, they will be enabled to do great things with their lives.

I have heard it said that liberation comes through education. And this is exactly what is happening in the lives of students in the GFA Bridge of Hope program. This is the liberation needed for the masses who live in South Asia.

I was surprised when I saw the cover of a *Time* magazine in 2006, calling India the next great economic superpower.[4] The sad reality is that this statement is only partially true. Although India as a whole is getting richer, the wealth of the nation is becoming

Armed with the knowledge that they have great value in the eyes of their loving Creator, these children can break the chains that have enslaved them all their lives.

increasingly concentrated in the hands of the educated minority, the high-castes who can afford to send their children to school and to college. You will almost never see a Dalit on a plane heading to the United States or to Germany to study information technology or to get an advanced degree as a lawyer, doctor or engineer. The vast majority of them are still working in the fields and factories.

This is why GFA Bridge of Hope is so important. Education enables these children to become leaders and strong, upstanding citizens, people who will be able to serve and lead their country in the years to come. Through education, liberty won't be limited to the hands of the few.

Hear the dream of one young girl.
Jassi's Dream
www.nolongeraslumdog.org

I heard the story of one young girl who is quickly blossoming into a brilliant student and leader, although she grew up in a situation that could only be described as critical. Without the intervention of the Lord through our GFA Bridge of Hope, it is hard to know what would have happened to her.

My name is Angeline. My mother was sick when I was born. I remember seeing her in her bed with big, big sores all over her body. She was always in pain. My father left us and married someone else. And then my mother died. I was 4 years old when this happened.

My grandmother decided she would take care of me, and she did until she also died when I was 6. I could not express the sorrow that I felt.

My aunt and her husband then decided to take me in. I lived in their home with their two children. It was a small room for all five of us, and we often only ate once in the day. I was so very sad then. I used to keep mum. I would not talk to anyone.

I was so scared and very sad when my aunt became sick too. I was certain that she would die and leave me.

Then something different happened. A man came and prayed for my aunt, and she got better. She decided to follow the Lord Jesus and enrolled me in a Bridge of Hope center.

When I first came, I would not talk to anybody. I would just sit in the corner by myself.

But eventually my heart was warmed. I saw the love of the people there. The women at the center were so nice and would always show me kindness.

I learned many new things at this center. My favorite verse in the Bible is James 1:5, where God says that whoever lacks wisdom should ask Him for it. So I ask God for wisdom, and He gives it to me. I started to do well in school, and now I get the best grades in my class.

I also love the Bible stories, like David and Goliath, and singing songs.

I know that I have changed a lot. I was so quiet when I came, but now I love to share with the other children—especially the ones who are quiet or hurting.

I feel so special to know that God loves me, and I pray to Him often. I pray for the Bridge of Hope center. I pray for people who are traveling, but most of all, I pray for all the people who are sick.

When I grow up, I want to tell other people about Jesus. I want to share Him with the ones who are hurting or alone or poor and sick. He has changed my life, and I want Him to change other people's lives too.

The Lord rescued Angeline, and I have no doubt that she will someday be a great and godly woman. Those who run the GFA Bridge of Hope center say she has excellent leadership potential. This girl who was not in school only a few years prior is now excelling tremendously, and her grades are some of the best in the class. She regularly shares the love of God with many other children in her village. Angeline's dreams are great, and with the

See Angeline flourishing at a GFA Bridge of Hope center.

 Angeline's Story: Before and After
www.nolongeraslumdog.org

knowledge that Jesus loves her, there is no telling where her impact will end.

As I was writing this chapter, my assistant sent me a link to a story that appeared in *The Telegraph,* a daily newspaper published in Calcutta. The story shocked me to tears.

On January 7, 2011, more than 50 women from a tribal village in Malda, West Bengal, got together to sell their children at the market. First I thought it was a misprint. People go to market to sell vegetables and material things, not to sell their *children!* As I read on, however, I learned that their entire village is impoverished. None of these women were able to care for their children anymore. The article continued:

> Among the women was Malati Hembram who had lined up with her five-year-old daughter. "I will sell her off at whatever price I get. The money is not important; I just want my daughter to be taken in by a family which will give her food, shelter and education. We are not being able to sustain ourselves as well as our children and the elders in the family," Malati said.[5]

I don't know if any of these women actually sold their children. If someone offered these mothers money, I think they would have done so. Sadly, I read on that it is not an uncommon sight to see women going from door-to-door trying to find a buyer for their son or daughter.

I have seen stories of deprivation, misery and hopelessness, but this one caught me completely unprepared. Immediately, I called our field leader nearest to this village, a man who was living more than 200 kilometers away from them. I told him, "We need to set up a center in this village right away."

Within one week, I got a call back from our leader saying that they had established a GFA Bridge of Hope center with 150 of these desperately hungry children. They distributed blankets and met some basic needs of the poor people in the village. And now these children would be cared for, get a warm meal each day and receive an education. As it often happens, a door was opened for our workers to share the love of Christ and bring the assurance that God will take care of them. Thank God that we were able to learn about their situation before it was too late.

God knows. He hears. He sees their pain. And He has brought us to the point at which we can, by His grace, help do something about it.

"I can't imagine being a parent and having to watch my child suffer because I'm not able to provide for them. I want to ease that suffering for both the parents and child."

—Mr. and Mrs. E.M.,
    GFA Bridge of Hope sponsor,
    Saint Louis, Missouri

How far that little candle throws his beams! So shines a good deed in a naughty world.

William Shakespeare, *The Merchant of Venice*[1]

CHAPTER FIVE

$\mathcal{I}$t is $\mathcal{H}$appening

An illiterate man came with a strange request to our GFA Bridge of Hope leaders: Would they send the "medical doctor named Jesus" to help his sick wife? He was dead serious and quite desperate in his pleading.

Here is the story. In a GFA Bridge of Hope center in Northeast India, a first grader named Nibun was not only getting a normal education in mathematics, reading and writing, but he was also learning about Jesus. He listened closely as his teachers talked about this man healing the sick, casting out demons and feeding the hungry.

Nibun's home was a mud hut where he lived with his parents. Like other poor families, they didn't have the luxury of going to a hospital when they were sick; it was simply too expensive and most doctors were several miles away. Five or ten miles may not seem like much while riding in a car or a bus, but it's a long distance to travel on a dirt path through the woods, especially when sick.

Nibun's mother had been very ill. His father did everything he could and even cried out to all his gods for help. But she continued to get worse, and soon her situation became critical. That's when Nibun told his father about the amazing things Jesus did. And this poor man thought we had a medical doctor named Jesus at our GFA Bridge of Hope center.

In response to his request, two missionaries went to extend whatever help they could. They talked with the family about Jesus and explained the Gospel. Finally, they laid hands on the woman and prayed that God would heal her.

Just as we read in the Word of God, the Lord in His mercy did just that. The news spread like wildfire throughout the small village. Through this miracle, several others came to know the Lord. The following week, more families placed their faith in Jesus.

To understand how incredible this is, it's important to know that this particular community had earlier shown no interest whatsoever in hearing the Good News. It was not until Nibun's mother was healed that they wanted to know more.

Subsequently, the first church in the history of this community was soon established. Now the life-changing Gospel continues to spread to neighboring villages, and more people are coming to know the saving power of Christ.

See how God brings new life to a family.
Nibun's Story
www.nolongeraslumdog.org

Think about it. What if Nibun was given a good education, plenty of food, clothes and all the same physical benefits we had provided him, *but* never had a chance to learn about the Lord Jesus Christ and the Word of God; what would have happened?

Would he have been able to tell his father about the "medical doctor named Jesus" who healed his mother? How many people would have come to know the Lord that day? Perhaps there would be no church in that village. Without the liberating power of Christ's love, how many people would still be living with the mindset of being trapped, worthless and hopeless?

It is so important that we do not look at physical assistance alone as "fulfilling" the Great Commission. If our goal is simply to improve people's outward status without touching their soul, then we are no different than any of the hundreds of other relief organizations out there today.

The miraculous awakening in this village all began with one little boy named Nibun learning about the Lord for the first time in his life in a GFA Bridge of Hope center.

And his story is not an exception; it is becoming almost a daily occurrence.

THEY FIND HOPE

My eyes fill with tears of joy when I think of the tens of thousands of dear children in our centers. Through our national missionaries who serve in these marginalized communities, children find hope in Jesus.

Beacons of life and healing, GFA Bridge of Hope centers are facilities established in a community where up to 200 children are able to come every day. We provide a holistic approach to their development, focusing on three main areas: the child's physical, mental and spiritual growth.

Physical Needs

A GFA Bridge of Hope center is tailored to meet the specific physical needs of the children in each center. For example, our nutrition specialists determine what food and vitamins are needed at each center and fix a daily meal accordingly. In addition, for each student, GFA Bridge of Hope provides a uniform, a backpack and school supplies like pencils and books.

Being able to eat every day is no longer a luxury for the many children in GFA Bridge of Hope.

Furthermore, as the staff observes the children, they can learn what other items the children need—things like toothpaste and towels that many of the children have either never heard of or never even considered using before.

These physical necessities were in desperate need in Tamil Nadu and Sri Lanka after the devastating tsunami in 2004. It tore through South Asia, killing an estimated 200,000 people, flattening whole villages and leaving more than a million people homeless.[2]

There was a young woman named Mariyam whose life was almost destroyed by the monster waves. Before it hit, her husband made about Rs. 500 per day (US$11.00) selling fish. The family ate well, and the children were able to attend school. But that was before he lost all his fishing boats. Without the boats, there was no income.

Her husband went to his parents for help, but they refused because Mariyam was of a lower caste than they were. When he returned home, beside himself with grief, he did the unthinkable; he committed suicide by dousing himself with kerosene and setting himself on fire.

Mariyam was left in shock. She was now a widow with a lame foot, an infant daughter, two school-age boys and no income. She did what she could to sell odds and ends but only made about Rs. 10–20 (maybe 30 cents) a day. The family was not surviving.

That's when the Lord sent a sister from the local church to visit her. She shared the love of Christ, and Mariyam, hearing there was a God who loved her in the midst of this suffering, received Jesus into her heart. She started to attend church and learned about GFA Bridge of Hope.

Her sons were admitted into the GFA Bridge of Hope program, where their tuition was paid and they received help with their studies. They were also fed a wholesome meal every day, which was something their mother wasn't able to provide. Because the boys had no father, the staff at the center took special care of them. For the first time in their lives, the two brothers heard songs and stories about Jesus. Now the whole family has drawn close to the Lord through the care and provision of our GFA Bridge of Hope.

Mariyam's son Kavisan shares about finding hope after the tsunami.

 Kavisan's Life: From Tsunami to Hope
www.nolongeraslumdog.org

Healthy Living

Part of the curriculum taught at the centers is on health and hygiene. We teach children the importance of washing their hands after using the facilities and before they eat, as well as taking a bath regularly. Every year they get a medical checkup. This is the first time many of these children have seen a doctor.

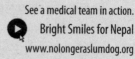

See a medical team in action.
Bright Smiles for Nepal
www.nolongeraslumdog.org

As we sit in our homes with indoor plumbing, central air and plenty of blankets, it's hard to imagine how the simple act of bathing can have an eternal impact on someone's life. But that's exactly what happened in one of our centers in West Bengal.

At that GFA Bridge of Hope center, there were two unruly boys named Deepan and Chitral. Although their father was opposed to the Christian faith, he still enrolled his children in the center so they could get an education. This family was poor and knew almost nothing about hygiene. Because of this, the two brothers had sores all over their bodies when they first came to the center.

The GFA Bridge of Hope staff started to bathe the boys with warm water. They talked to the parents about hygiene, but they did not want to listen. Nevertheless, the staff would apply medicine and dress the boys' sores. Through this care and prayer, the boys were healed.

As time went by, Deepan and Chitral became more disciplined, and their parents took notice. At home, the brothers would sing songs they learned at the center. They would pray before meals and prior to studying.

Both their father and mother were amazed. Gradually their hearts opened to the Gospel and they decided to follow Jesus. Now the whole family is attending church regularly. This story is not uncommon; there are many parents, neighbors and relatives whose lives have changed as a result of a GFA Bridge of Hope center being present in their village.

Academic Excellence

Year after year, the children from GFA Bridge of Hope consistently get high marks in their classes. There are GFA Bridge of Hope students who achieve first rank and first class. GFA Bridge of Hope students are regularly among the highest-scoring children in the state of Nepal and throughout India. How does this happen?

The students at our GFA Bridge of Hope centers learn good study habits from the teachers who work with them. They have adequate time to ask questions, get tutoring and learn how to think creatively. Children are encouraged to pray to the Lord for wisdom and understanding in their schooling. Thus they improve in school and receive higher marks on their exams. This boosts their confidence and encourages them to keep attending.

One young lad named Ghalib was an unruly child who disobeyed and found it difficult to concentrate on anything. He would fight with his parents even as they would fight with each other.

Then his mother found out about GFA Bridge of Hope and enrolled Ghalib, forcing him to attend. In his own words, he "found something new."

Through the attentive tutelage he received, he learned to pay attention to his studies and began to succeed in school. He also learned about the love of Jesus and started to value his new opportunity. He has memorized Psalm 23 by heart and often prays to the Lord. When asked about his experience, Ghalib said, "Really, God has blessed my family and me."

Lessons for Life

In addition to the lessons about discipline and study, the children also learn biblical moral values such as the importance

Children learn vital skills such as discipline, hygiene and manners. They become more respectful and courteous and are more willing to study and help their parents at home.

of respecting parents and elders, of telling the truth and of not being willfully disobedient. This transformation in attitude and behavior is quickly noticed by parents.

Padimni's parents came to our GFA Bridge of Hope center to thank the teachers for the change they saw in their daughter. The girl had been a thief most of her life, often stealing food from her family and money from her father. But one day at the GFA Bridge of Hope center, she heard about Jesus, and it changed her completely. Padimni listened carefully to a lesson taught about stealing. She learned that stealing was wrong and that she should change her behavior. So she did.

Another child, a boy named Isar, was constantly fighting with the neighboring boys. His parents warned him that he wouldn't have any friends because of his actions. And they were right; Isar found himself without any friends.

Then he met two new boys who were enrolled in a GFA Bridge of Hope center nearby. They befriended him, even though he was an angry child. He asked his mother if he could go to the center too, so she enrolled him.

The changes in Isar were swift and dramatic. His parents didn't hear complaints about his negative behavior anymore. Isar made many friends and learned to respect his parents and his elders. His whole nature and attitude changed.

Spiritual Lessons

One of the most amazing things to hear about is how God is revealing Himself to these children. As they hear the Word of the Lord and encounter His love at the centers, the Holy Spirit works in the hearts of these young ones, showing them God's faithfulness. It is beautiful to see children offer up their prayers to the Lord and to witness their joy at His amazing responses.

Rinvi is a perfect example. This young girl was more interested in hearing about Jesus than in playing games. She would remember the details of all the stories she heard.

Her grandfather, who lived with her family, could not see. They had tried everything they could, including an operation, but nothing helped. Then one day Rinvi remembered a story about a blind man whom Jesus healed. Because of this, she believed the Lord was also able to heal her grandfather.

When she got home that day, she boldly told her grandfather that the Lord was able to heal him. Then she asked him to close his eyes, and she prayed for him to be healed. As she prayed, he regained his eyesight.

After this miracle, Rinvi's faith began to grow. One day she was stuck at the GFA Bridge of Hope center because of heavy

The children learn to pray while at GFA Bridge of Hope, and it is beautiful to see how God answers their requests time and time again. Their faith in Him grows as He heals the sick, changes lives and performs miracles.

rains, so she prayed for the rain to stop. And it did.

Another girl, Madhari, wanted God to heal her dad because he had been vomiting for two days. She prayed for him, and God healed him!

Then there was a little boy named Balaji; he was only 5 years old!

At his GFA Bridge of Hope center, he heard stories about God's miraculous healings. So when he and his friend both caught a fever, he prayed that night to be healed so he could go back to school. The next morning he woke up in perfect health and was surprised that his friend was still sick! So later that night Balaji told his buddy that he needed to ask Jesus for his healing too.

It amazes me how beautifully simple the faith of these children is. God said it, so it must be true. They memorize Scriptures, whole psalms and chapters, as well as action songs and Bible stories.

Children learn by the example they see, and when given a good example to follow, they will take it and run with it. This is what happened in one GFA Bridge of Hope center in West Bengal.

Sagen is an 8-year-old boy who lives in a poor village where there is no electricity. Most of the people there labor in the fields around their homes.

At the center where Sagen attends, the children frequently see the staff praying about various matters. The staff also encourages the children to pray for each other. They have formed prayer groups and can be seen almost every day, whether in school or out, praying for each other's needs. Sagen is the leader of one such group that has attained quite the reputation.

Sagen and several other children found out about a boy named Santanu Malik, who had been sick for several years. He lived in the next village over. The boy's mother was so distressed about his illness that she thought, *If I can, I'll go inside the earth or I'll go above the sky to flee from this situation.*

Her son had a tumor in his brain that left him unable to walk. Sometimes the right side of his body would twitch violently, and he wasn't able to eat much. Sagen and the boys visited Santanu many times to pray for him, but nothing seemed to be happening. Still they persisted. Then one day Santanu was suddenly healed! He even went outside to play with his new friends.

Since then, Sagen and his young "prayer partners" have been called on to pray for many other people in the village. When Sagen's grandfather became ill with stomach pains, he simply said, "Sagen, you know how to pray. Would you please pray for me?" The next day his grandfather told him, "Because of your prayers, I got healed."

Witness the incredible power of children's prayer.
▶ The Power of the Meek
www.nolongeraslumdog.org

It has gotten to the point that whenever anyone in the village gets sick, they call for the boys on this prayer team. God is using these boys' prayers to open up many hearts to Himself.

Sagen continues to pray because as he puts it, "Really, it's so amazing to speak with the Creator of all! And when we pray to Jesus, we feel good in our hearts."

I am overwhelmed when little children like this get involved in the work of the Lord! No wonder Jesus said, "I tell you the truth, unless you change and become like little children, you will never enter the kingdom of heaven" (Matthew 18:3). We have much to learn from these young ones.

Families Flourish

Parents of the children in our GFA Bridge of Hope centers often tell us of amazing things that happen in their homes through their kids. The children act as the conduit of God's love, teaching their parents what they have learned.

Here is the story of one such family that was changed by their son's involvement in a GFA Bridge of Hope center. The boy's father, Rajiv, relates what happened.

After attending the Bridge of Hope center, my son used to come home and say, "This is what my sir said, and this is what our teacher taught us." Regarding spiritual life, regarding our way of living and regarding our health and hygiene, he would come and tell us. It was kind of exciting! So, when my son says something to me, for example, about hygiene, I am changing.

Some of the things he says about prayer and about Jesus really touch me. Slowly by slowly, I am changing according to what he says to us.

The Bridge of Hope really brought a kind of revival in me spiritually. Basically I'm an illiterate person. I do not know how to read and write. Many times my son would come and say words he learned at the Bridge of Hope center. "This is what the Word of God says." So many times when we would do wrong things, the Word of God would speak to us. And because it was the Word of God speaking, we changed a lot.

We have prayer every day in our home for 15 to 20 minutes. My son reads the Bible, and we sing some songs. Now Jesus is the main focus of our life. We cannot leave Jesus and go anywhere, because Jesus is with us and He guides us every day. This kind of spiritual awareness, through my son, I got through Bridge of Hope.

Children take their newfound joy home with them and share it with their parents.

Children aren't the only ones who are transformed. Their parents watch their conduct and learn of the Lord from them, and their lives are also impacted. I remember hearing of one little boy named Ruhan and how the Lord intervened in the lives of his parents and saved them from making a terrible decision.

Ruhan showed up at his GFA Bridge of Hope center one morning in tears, having just learned that his parents were going to file for divorce that very day. He poured out his heart to one of the staff members. When they realized what was going on, the leader and the social worker at the center rushed to the courthouse to do some last-minute marital counseling.

Because of problems they were having, Ruhan's parents had decided to divorce. The two staff members were able to counsel them and to help them understand the importance of restoring their broken marriage, not only for themselves but also for their son.

Through the intervention, prayers and counseling of the staff, Ruhan's parents recommitted themselves to accept each other and live together.

As they learned more about Christ, his parents' hearts knit back together. Now they have a strong marriage, and the whole family is growing in the saving knowledge of the Lord. His peace in their lives is evident to all.

COMMUNITY DEVELOPMENT

Like with Nibun, the little boy whose father thought Jesus was a doctor, the healing touch of a GFA Bridge of Hope center extends into the whole community. The children individually take home what they have learned to their parents, and the staff of a GFA Bridge of Hope open up the center and invite people in as well.

Our trained staff is able to help villagers struggling with issues such as alcoholism and family strife. Through prayer and counsel, entire villages have been transformed. No longer places of hopelessness, these villages are filled with joyful, caring people who finally have a reason for living.

We work hard to bless the community in numerous ways. A center may offer workshops open to everyone on a health care issue or put on a presentation for a holiday. GFA Bridge of Hope centers also sponsor "community days" in which the staff goes out and cleans the village gutters and bus stops.

We drill "Jesus Wells" that provide pure water for those who would otherwise have to walk great distances or for people denied access because of their caste. There are literacy programs, vocational training and micro-financing, all to enable poor men and women to escape the poverty and oppression in which they have been trapped for several millennia.

The medical clinics we provide are often attended by the entire village. There are so many who need help that sometimes people stand in line all day just to be seen!

Gospel for Asia has a catalog we put out every Christmas with various items like sewing machines, water filters, goats, chickens and rickshaws that people with financial means can buy for people in Asia. The social workers at the GFA Bridge of Hope centers know the poor families in the community who would most benefit from the free gift of a cow or a fishing net. These items show Christ's love in a tangible way, while they are also tools to help break the cycle of poverty that is so prevalent in Dalit and low-caste communities.

Within all of these programs, we have seen that helping kids is the largest bridge to bring hope to a family, a village or a people.

The staff of the GFA Bridge of Hope centers are able to counsel the parents, as was the case with the boy Ruhan, and give them a new perspective on life. Health is improved as previously ignorant villagers learn about sanitation, like with Deepan and Chitral. The prayers of the children are answered by the Almighty God, as He heard the cries of Rinvi, Balaji and Sagen. Children like Padimni and Isar blossom into well-behaved students who excel in their studies. Each one of these children impacted their community and is a testimony to the transformational power of the Lord.

As people come to know the Lord and experience life as He offers it, whole communities are radically changed. Suddenly there is grace, there is peace and there is a supernatural love that people have for one another. Even tribes that had been engaged in bloody conflicts for as long as anyone can remember are suddenly meeting together to worship the Lord in unity.

It is impossible to tell the full extent of what the Lord is doing in Asia today; there is no one person who knows all of it! However, the events going on in one community in Uttar Pradesh are a highlight of the awesome work of the Lord.

When we first went to this community, we were struck with the hopelessness and oppressive atmosphere in which the people lived. The children were uneducated, hardly dressed and sick from easily preventable causes like having no clean water to drink or a vitamin deficiency. The parents and their children toiled all hours of the day or didn't work at all and went hungry. Many of the men would come home and abuse their wives and children, wasting their money on drugs and alcohol. They knew nothing of the genuine love of Christ.

For the past several years, Gospel for Asia has been focusing our efforts to show Christ's love to these hurting people. This has been done through drilling Jesus Wells, setting up GFA Bridge of Hope centers, holding one-day medical clinics, establishing literacy programs for the women and basically doing all we can to help these people better survive the harsh circumstances into which they were born.

It has been simply astounding to see what God has done! In this one community alone, 2,000 families came to know the love of Christ and decided to follow Him! For the first time, their children are getting an education, and their mothers are learning how to read. Hundreds of husbands who used to be drunkards and abusive to their families have become decent, honest men. There is a renewing of their minds, their hearts are warmed toward each other, and the people are starting to care for others, not just themselves.

The people there have seen how hard we have tried to be of help and to love them in the midst of the depravity in which they live. They want to know, "Why are you doing this? What is it about your God that would cause you to help us?"

These stories have been repeated over and over. By the grace of God, there are hundreds of testimonies like this. Physical assistance alone cannot account for the amazing transformation that we have seen in these villages. There is only one way we can explain it: *The Holy Spirit is moving in Asia.*

IT IS HAPPENING

Lift up your eyes. Children are being fed, clothed and loved. They are getting an education like no one in their family ever did before. Thousands of them are experiencing the love of Christ. There are more than 60,000 children enrolled in GFA Bridge of Hope centers (as of March 2011), but what is that number compared to the millions who are still wandering without hope?

The opportunity is astounding. Never before have so many people in Asia been so open to the message of love found in the

Gospel. As followers of Christ, we must respond while we can.

Someone once said, "Harvest is a fixed time." In my village in India, there are hundreds of farmers. My own brothers are farmers. When harvest time comes, no one goes on vacation. No one says, "Let's go away for a month and enjoy life; then we'll come back and do the work." Why?

Because within a few weeks time, the rain will begin to fall. The season will change, and the entire harvest will be destroyed if it is not brought in. We must never say, "Later . . . tomorrow . . . next month . . . two years from now I'll be part of the harvest." The opportunity will be gone.

The need is almost overwhelming. The sheer numbers drive us to our knees. But don't be daunted by the size of the task; you *can* make a difference in the life of a child.

In some parts of the world, when the tide comes in from the ocean, it brings with it thousands of starfish. Then the tide recedes and leaves thousands of them behind on the shore. Many of these starfish cannot make it back to the safety of the water before the sun comes up and dries them out.

A man was walking along the shore one day and witnessed this sight. He stared at all the starfish, saddened that so many would die.

Then he saw a young boy walking in the other direction. The lad would stop and pick up a starfish and throw it into the ocean. He continued to do this, picking up one after the other and throwing them back into the water.

"Why are you doing that?" the man asked the boy. "Don't you realize there are miles and miles of shore? You're wasting your time. You'll never make a difference."

The boy simply picked up another starfish and hurled it back into the ocean. As it landed, he said, "I made a difference for that one."

Like the young boy, we cannot save them all. But you and I *can* make a difference. Let's not let what we can't do stop us from doing what we can do.

 "I see the faces of these precious children and my heart goes out to them. I like to think that one person can make a difference, even if it is only one child at a time."

—Ms. M.L.,
GFA Bridge of Hope sponsor,
Saltsburg, Pennsylvania

Every man feels instinctively that all the beautiful sentiments in the world weigh less than a single lovely action.

James Russell Lowell[1]

CHAPTER SIX

W<small>HAT</small> N<small>OW</small>?

A few years ago while speaking at a conference in Los Angeles, I talked about the plight of the suffering Dalits and the hopelessness of their children. Some of the statistics shocked my audience, such as the fact that there are 50 million child laborers in India alone[2] or that 1.2 million children are trafficked as slaves and prostitutes every single year.[3]

At the end of the session, a man came up and handed me a CD, saying, "You will want to listen to the song, 'What Now.' You'll like it." The CD was by the musician Steven Curtis Chapman.[4]

I listened to the song later that day, and his lyrics moved me to tears.

Through the song, you find yourself face-to-face with an orphaned little girl on "the other side of world," destitute, just looking at you. The Lord steps in and basically says, "I am that girl." And His question then hangs in the air: *What now?*

I must warn you, my reader—you can no longer say you didn't know. Through this book, you've seen their faces. I am sure you have felt their pain.

The question I need to ask is—and I ask on behalf of these children and the God who cares for them—what will you do now?

Like me, I believe you want to save them. I think you've heard their pleas for help, and you hope there is something you can do to rescue them.

I want to inform you that there is a way, and you can be part of the rescue party. Please join with us as we continue to build this "bridge of hope" for the children of southern Asia.

The path of their life is completely changed by these children's involvement in a GFA Bridge of Hope center.

It has already become evident that the Lord greatly desires to see these young lives reached, and He has given us this unique privilege to join Him in a great harvest. Let us take advantage of this opportunity to get involved in His awesome work.

PRAY

When you see these photos of children or hear the stories of what they have suffered, don't let heartbreak and compassion be the extent of your response; begin to *pray*. There is nothing so crucial to our ministry as prayer. As Sir Thomas Buxton said, "You know the value of prayer; it is precious beyond all price. Never, never neglect it."[5]

As you read in earlier chapters, God answers when His people call out to Him. Pray for the children you see and read about. If you don't know the name of a given child, make up a name. God knows whom you are speaking to Him about and will do His work to change that life.

For some time, our staff has been praying against the sexual assaults that happen to little girls in Asia. Recently, we were encouraged to hear this story of how God has answered.

In Sri Lanka, there was a village of laborers who lived in shanty homes. Every night, men from the neighboring areas would come and rape the young girls. There was nothing the laborers could do to stop them. The poor workers lived in constant fear.

When one of our missionaries found out about this situation, he went to the authorities. They responded, assuring protection for the people. Furthermore, they allowed the missionary, Pastor Sampath, his wife and several women from the church to minister to the people of this village. They now give the children baths, trim their fingernails, feed them balanced meals and pass out clothes to wear. The Lord is working. I believe He heard our prayers for these little girls.

You too can literally change lives by praying. God is ready to answer. Remember the story of Nadish and how the Lord rescued him?

If you want ideas of what to pray for, go to our website, www. gfa.org/slumdog/pray. You will see numerous children and families to pray for. Look at their pictures. Read their stories. Listen to their songs.

Ever since we started more than 30 years ago, Gospel for Asia has always been a ministry with prayer as the focus. We intercede on behalf of

Listen to Ahanti sing.
Ahanti: A New Song of Hope
www.nolongeraslumdog.org

the lost world every Tuesday night and the first Friday of every month. Likewise, I encourage you to pray. If there is a prayer team that meets at your church, join them and add your faith to theirs. If there is not, why not start your own prayer group? Invite everyone you can, no matter their age. When we have special prayer requests, we ask the children at our home office to pray—and it happens! God answers.

I wrote a brochure about how to have an effective and lively prayer meeting. This brochure, *Guidelines to Effective Prayer Meetings,* can be downloaded for free online. Please make prayer a regular part of your life and be confident that God hears and answers. You will be blessed also as you come before the Lord and seek His face.

BRING THEM HOPE

I encourage you to take yet another step.

You can have a direct impact on the life of a child through our GFA Bridge of Hope ministry. You will have a specific child to intercede on behalf of, a young boy or girl somewhere in Asia. The money you give, just US$35 a month, will provide that child with food, clothing, school supplies and an education. He or she will get medical checkups every year and at last have a safe place to laugh and grow. But most important, your sponsored child will learn about the love of Christ, the One who transforms lives.

To sponsor a GFA Bridge of Hope child, tear out the sponsorship card and send it in to Gospel for Asia. Alternately, you can go to our website, www.gfa.org/slumdog, and prayerfully look through the pictures. God will guide you to a child.

Instead of a future where she is forced to provide for her family through backbreaking physical labor, this child will go on to receive a higher education, becoming an engineer or possibly a teacher.

Once you become a sponsor, you then have the incredible privilege of praying for and writing to your child. You will receive his or her prayers and letters in return. Your child will never forget you or what you have done.

Remember, too, that your chosen child will not be the only one whose life is transformed. I am constantly amazed how the Lord works not only in the hearts of individuals but also in communities, transforming many lives through a single GFA Bridge of Hope center. As if that were not enough, the families of the people who sponsor these children are also radically changed. One by one the stories reach us, revealing God's special providence in each situation.

There were two young brothers, ages 7 and 5, who were learning about Asia. They were especially touched when they heard about the needs of many of the children there. Their parents started reading to them my first book, *Revolution in World Missions,* and the boys were eager to help in whatever way they could. Their parents showed them our website so they could get personally involved.

The boys prayed for several days, asking God to help them choose a child to sponsor. Then they spent about an hour online searching through the children until they announced they had found one. He was a boy just about their age.

In order to pay for the child, they started their own "cookie company." They have been baking them every week since. I'm told their house smells like it too! The two boys hope to make enough money to soon start sponsoring another child.

Their parents have said, "What a blessing it is to see God working in the hearts of our own children as they reach out to serve others."

Spread the Word

We can all learn from the example of these two young boys. In order to sell their cookies, I imagine they have had opportunities to tell their extended family and neighbors about their GFA Bridge of Hope child.

Likewise, you can be a part of the rescue team by spreading the word. This book is an excellent resource to open people's eyes to this reality, and you can order more copies to give to your friends or relatives.

We have other books as well. If you haven't already, I encourage you to read my first book, *Revolution in World Missions*. It tells of the origins of Gospel for Asia and the work of our national missionaries. You can get a copy at www.gfa.org/store.

But don't stop with your immediate family; share what you are doing with your friends, relatives, co-workers and church members. Explain why you are doing it and how they too can get involved.

Simple Living

Many people find the idea of sponsoring a child to be an incredible eye-opener. They come to appreciate the blessings they have and start to recognize that they own much more than they need. Just the cost of coffee, of going out to eat, of the latest fashions, T-shirts, CDs and DVDs, or even of that special candy you love so much can literally save a child in Asia.

Often I go through my closet and remove all the clothes I don't wear. I don't need them. I drive around in a 1962 yellow

Volkswagen bug—it still works! I remember in the early days of the ministry when God convicted me about how much money I spent on chewing gum.

Please don't misunderstand. I'm not saying that a nice car or new clothes or anything like that is a bad thing. If poverty made us more spiritual, then there would be a lot of really spiritual people all over South Asia. No. This is about seeing the little ways that the Lord calls us to live simply so that others might simply live.

God reveals to people all over the world about the small sacrifices they can make in His name. In one instance, there was a mother who used to spend $30 every month to buy a special makeup she loved. She knew in her heart that it was only a fleeting thing, and she wanted to invest in something with eternal value. The Lord had been telling her family to die to the cares of this world and to take up their cross and follow Him. So they did, and He led them to support a GFA Bridge of Hope child. Together with her two sons, ages 7 and 9, she picked out a child to sponsor and pray for. Her boys even gave $2, the only money they had. As they pray together and write to their child, it's been a great way to bond as a family.

I recall another family that downgraded their cable subscription so that they could sponsor two children. Their hope was to teach their own children to enjoy giving more than receiving. They could honestly say, "What a difference [Gospel for Asia] is making in the lives of children . . . including our own."

One little girl gave "lots of money" to sponsor another young girl in Asia. Her words were, "I am almost 5 years old, and I saw the little children who had no clothes, food, dolls or anything and had to dig in the garbage. So I got out lots of money to give to them. I want them to have a doll of their own. I love the little girl I saw."

Perhaps because these children are still so young, they can empathize with someone who has lost their mother or wonder what it would be like not to have food to eat or toys to play with. And they have not learned to ignore what they see.

The words of one girl changed the course of someone on the other side of the world, and she was only 3 years old. Her parents heard about GFA's Christmas catalog while listening to a spot on the radio. They came to our website, www.gfa.org/gift, to give a goat. Then they got a copy of my first book, and their eyes were opened to our national missionary program, so they sponsored three missionaries. After that, they found out about GFA Bridge of Hope.

Soon, they sat with their young daughter in front of the computer, looking through the children's pictures. The parents chose to sponsor a little boy. Then they continued to look further through the profiles. That's when their little daughter spoke up and pointed to a young girl. Her parents clicked on her, and their daughter laughed and smiled, saying, "Now we have picked a boy and a girl!"

Her parents had not intended to sponsor two children that night. So they asked their little daughter, "Which one should we sponsor, the boy or the girl?"

She said, "Both of them." And they could think of no reason why not to.

Our Privilege

You know the need, the opportunity and the urgency. What now? I pray you will not say, "I need to think about it," or "I'm too busy right now. I'll do it later," or a dozen other excuses.

Procrastination is a deadly enemy. We mean well. We may know we are prompted by God to do something, but somehow we forget about it. Our lives become busy, and somehow our "good intentions" drop to the bottom of our to-do lists.

But there is something you can do right now to bring hope to the least of these: pray, spread the word and sponsor a child. Make a choice to love them as Christ does.

Please help us reach out and save these children.

It's my heart's cry: *Lord, help us rescue at least 500,000 children*

A "bridge of hope" is being built, one child at a time, spanning the generations to reach millions upon millions of people who were born into hopelessness. These are people Christ loves, people He died to save.

from despair and hopelessness. Together, we can give them hope.

Sponsoring a child is one of the most fulfilling joys. I know of one man who was particularly blessed when he was able to meet one of the dozens of children that he and his family sponsor. This is his story, and he tells it with tears.

My name is Jim. My beautiful wife and I have been sponsoring children since we first found out about Gospel for Asia's Bridge of Hope program. We had always wanted to have a large family, perhaps a dozen children, but our hearts were changed as we saw the incredible need of the poor children throughout Asia.

Instead of a dozen, we have had two children. Then we got four more through GFA Bridge of Hope. They are our little hearts, children whose letters we read over and over again. Their pictures are mounted on our wall, and every day the four of us pray for them. I consider them to be my children and love them as my own, although I was sure we would never meet this side of eternity.

But God blew my socks off and sent me to India on a business venture about a year ago. My wife reminded me about Gospel for Asia and said I should give them a call to see if I could visit a GFA Bridge of Hope center while I was there. Amazingly, I could!

My heart was not ready for the sight of India. Still, the images of people, I can only assume they were Dalits, sitting on the roadside without any life in their eyes . . . everything looked so hopeless! I felt incredibly burdened for these people. It almost brought me to tears to see them and still does to this day.

But when I went to the center, I was simply astonished! The joy! The laughter! The sight of these children, hundreds of them, beautiful, laughing, singing! It was so different from everything I saw around them. They were so vibrant and full of life!

This group of over 100 kids was laughing, studying and learning about the Lord all at once! It was amazing. But all of this did not prepare me for what was about to happen.

There was one little face in the crowd that I recognized. When I saw him, my little Manu, I just froze. The teacher told him who I was, and he locked eyes with me and he smiled the largest smile I have ever seen! He ran up to me and latched onto me like I was a life raft in the middle of the ocean.

This little 8-year-old boy stepped back and looked at me straight in the eyes. "Dad," he said, "thank you for loving me."

I burst into tears.

After that day, I have never been the same. I left India with a new perspective on life. Anything we could do to help these children, we must do.

Now my wife and I sponsor two dozen children—twice as many as we ever thought we would have as our own! They are scattered all throughout India and Nepal. I cannot imagine doing anything more worthwhile with my life. This is it. My family and I, we are dedicated to saving as many people as we can. And Gospel for Asia enables us to do it.

While we care for our own children, let us remember that there are millions walking on the streets, homeless and helpless. There are hundreds of millions more suffering in the remote villages. They live their lives in conditions we cannot fathom. Their little hearts suffer more pain than anyone should have to bear. Many children honestly believe they are worth less than a dog.

But you can help change that. You can bring hope to a little child.

Like in the movie *Slumdog Millionaire,* these children roam the streets. That's reality.

But now there is something you *can* do about it.

Please, go before the Lord.

He will tell you what to do.

"If we were in a position and couldn't provide these things for our children, I know I would hope that other Christians would step in and help if they were able . . . so that is what we are doing."

— Miss K.M.,
GFA Bridge of Hope sponsor,
Gilbert, Arizona

Nobody made a greater mistake than he who did nothing because he could do only a little.

Edmund Burke[1]

CHAPTER SEVEN

MAKE YOUR LIFE COUNT

Regrets. I've had a few in my life. There are times I said to myself, "If only . . ." or "I wish . . ." Like you, I feel sad for the past failures, mistakes and sins.

One of my most painful memories has to do with a little girl named Meena. Meena was a beautiful 5-year-old living in Bombay. She had the biggest brown eyes. When the social workers first saw her, she was standing in six inches of sewer water.

Meena was one of the thousands of children who survive by begging on the streets. No one knows if her parents abandoned her or simply died. Her life was sustained by the meager sums she could coax from passersby and the scraps she would often eat out of the garbage piles just to stay alive.

I saw a photo of Meena, and it's one I can never forget. Later, I learned that she began eating sewage-infested dirt off of the streets. Soon she went into a coma and died.

The sad thing is that there are still children eating dirt to fill their empty stomachs. They are silent victims of poverty, quietly passing unnoticed from some of the darkest places on earth.

For Meena it's too late. My deep regret is that we didn't have a GFA Bridge of Hope center in her slum to rescue her.

Children like Meena make it important, critically important, for us to move from "good intentions" to *actions*.

C.S. Lewis put it very well when he said, "The more often we feel without acting, the less we will be able ever to act, and, in the long run, the less we will be able to feel."[2]

We have now walked together through almost all the pages of this book. You have started to feel the pain and anguish of these forgotten lives. I assume your heart was touched as you read the real-life accounts of the Dalits, the OBCs and especially their precious children.

Please don't close your heart now. Don't start to numb the pain you feel for these suffering, helpless children. Please love them. Love them in Jesus' name.

You and I did not ask to be born and raised in the circumstances and comforts we have. You too could have been born destitute in one of the slums of Calcutta or in a Dalit family in Bihar. You could have been that little slumdog, blinded and turned into a street beggar. It's true, you might even have been sold into the sex business and died long before your 20th birthday.

God in His mercy gave us the privilege of living our lives with the freedom and blessings words can't describe. Just remember Jesus' words: "From everyone who has been given much, much will be required" (Luke 12:48, NASB).

There is no need to feel guilt and self-condemnation for the blessings we have. Instead, let us choose to see this challenge as an opportunity to be like Jesus in our generation.

I think you will agree, once in a while God tries to break into our normal lives and tell us something important. He brings a matter to our attention that tears at our hearts, maybe even brings us to our knees. But then, sadly, so often that is all that happens. Although it consumes us for a little while and we can't

These children now have hope.

stop thinking about it, eventually we start to explore something else and forget.

Because we see and hear so much nowadays, soon our hearts stop hurting. We get used to things as they are.

But that is not the way of Jesus.

Christ was the One who saw the multitudes and wept.

So many times as I learn and relearn the reality these children face, I again realize that for too long I missed something important. So I cry out, "Lord, what is wrong with me? How could I possibly forget?"

I get so caught up in my day-to-day activities that weeks and months and even years pass, and I don't realize how quickly they have gone.

Please don't get so involved in today's trivia that you forget eternity awaits us all. Keep in mind those who are captive in the worst sort of prisons because, "I tell you the truth, whatever you did for one of the least of these brothers of mine, you did for me" (Matthew 25:40). The opposite is also true: "Whatever you did not do for one of the least of these, you did not do for me" (Matthew 25:45).

It is for Jesus' sake that we act. It is in His name that we sacrifice.

Together, you and I, we can make dreams come true for precious children. We can and we must.

One of the earlier memories of my college days in the United States is about a television show starring George Burns. He looked old, really old. He wore these round glasses like Gandhi, whom I respect so much. He was always puffing a cigar in between his stories and songs.

There was something about him that I just liked. One thing was this song he sang, and he did it often. A few words really stuck with me, "I wish I was 18 again." (You can probably hear it on YouTube.)[3]

When the Lord called me to serve Him, I was barely 16! I was living in a tiny village in a small state at the southern tip of India. Today, as I am writing these lines, I am 60! And I think to myself, "Whatever happened to time?" It kind of feels like it was yesterday when I left my home, traveling 2,000 miles to northern India to serve the Lord.

How did time slip by so fast . . . I don't know!

Along with George Burns, I too feel like singing, "I wish I

was 18 again." Why? Because there is so much to be done. The world is broken, filled with so much suffering, so many precious children—all lost and helpless. I want to lead them to Jesus, the One who is their hope.

But I can't turn back the clock. Time flies by and before we know it, it's all over. There's the final good-bye from this earth and to all the things we thought were so important and held on to so tightly.

Think about it! One hundred years from now, what do they matter? The house, cars, clothes, pearls, bank accounts, vacations, real estate, opinions of others, honors we sought and lived for. Oh, how silly we are not to live in the light of eternity!

Now is our opportunity to see these precious people come to know the Lord. Amy Carmichael once said, "We shall have all eternity to celebrate the victories, but we have only the few hours before sunset in which to win them."[4]

What a day it is going to be when we stand before the throne to find multitudes that no man can number from every nation, every tribe and every tongue! Our willingness to work these few hours will make eternity that much richer.

I plead with you to stop and think about what I am saying. Take your ID card or your driver's license out and look at it. See your date of birth on it. How old are you now? Maybe 20, 40, 60 years—you know how old you are. Add 100 years to your present age. Where are you now? Where is your house? How much do the opinions of others matter to you?

You see what I am talking about.

Live in the light of eternity. Love God by loving others. Make your life count.

If you have been blessed by this book,
I would really like to hear from you.
Please send me an email at kp@gfa.org.

Give HOPE
to a child in
need today!

For †$35, you can provide a child in South Asia with education, nutritious meals, medical checkups—and the message of Jesus' love.

To begin sponsoring today, go to WWW.GFA.ORG/SLUMDOG

or complete the form below
or contact the GFA office nearest you.
(National office addresses are listed on page 166.)

GOSPEL FOR ASIA'S
BRIDGE OF HOPE

❏ Starting now, I will sponsor _____ Bridge of Hope children at †$35 each monthly for a total of $_____ per month. **(You'll receive a photo and biography of each child you sponsor.)**

❏ Please send me more information about sponsoring Bridge of Hope children.

Please circle: Mr. Mrs. Miss Rev.

Name

Address

City   State/Province

Zip/Postal Code   Country

Email   Phone (   )

HB52-RB9S

❏ I give Gospel for Asia permission to send me emails (i.e. field stories, urgent prayer requests, etc.).
❏ I give Gospel for Asia permission to send me text messages (i.e. urgent updates, etc.).

Privacy Policy: Gospel for Asia will not sell, lease or trade your personal information.

Gospel for Asia sends 100 percent of your child sponsorship pledge to the mission field. Nothing is taken out for administrative expenses.

†AUS $38 CAN $35 NZ $42 £23 ZA R250

FREQUENTLY ASKED QUESTIONS

I would like to be able to sit down with you and answer any questions that may have come up as you've read this book or discuss the plight of children in our generation. Who knows, maybe someday we will have such an opportunity. Until then, here are some questions people often ask—with their corresponding answers. You are always welcome to call or email our various national offices where we have people who can speak to the specific questions you may have.

I WANT TO GET INVOLVED. WHAT DO I DO?

Wonderful! I am glad the Lord has touched your heart with His concerns.

To sponsor a child, visit Gospel for Asia at www.gfa.org/slumdog, or call us at one of our offices listed on page 166.

The cost of sending a child to a GFA Bridge of Hope center is US$35/month. You can cover this by check or money order, or you can set up automatic withdrawals, a method that saves on the cost of paper and staffing needs.

After you sponsor a GFA Bridge of Hope student, you will receive a photo and information about your child, plus your first letter-writing kit. As soon as you do, or even before then, start to pray for your child and your child's family. Every six months or so, you should also receive a letter from the child you sponsor.

How can I pray for needy children in this world and for the Dalits?

My belief is that prayer is the most effective tool God has given us and is truly a means to change the world. As the Lord burdens your heart for needy Dalit children, remember that one of the main reasons why these people stay in bondage is the belief that this life is simply their lot. Pray for them to realize their great worth in God's eyes.

Pray for health and safety. God knows those in need and can provide for them as we ask Him.

Pray that the Lord will raise up more schools to benefit these children, their families and their communities. Pray for all people's hearts to be open to the Gospel. In every GFA Bridge of Hope center, each child has the opportunity to hear and understand how treasured he or she is in the eyes of God.

Pray for your child's adjustment to the GFA Bridge of Hope center. For many of the children, this is the first time they've ever attended school.

Pray for a supportive family and community. The initial response from parents could be negative, but over time, most fathers and mothers usually express sincere gratitude.

Pray for the Lord's will to be accomplished in each of these lives and that they will become an instrument of blessings to many.

Pray for a spiritual breakthrough all across Asia.

Be convinced that these children and the Dalits are on God's heart and that He is ready to answer our prayers if we but ask Him.

fold before tearing

YES! I WANT TO HELP CHILDREN IN ASIA

Dear Brother K.P., after reading *No Longer a Slumdog*, I've decided to bring the love of Jesus to GFA Bridge of Hope children today for $35 per month each. I understand that my pledge gift will provide a quality education, medical care, a daily meal and the chance for each sponsored child to know Jesus.

☐ **I will sponsor** _____ children at $35 each monthly for a total of $ _____ per month.

PLEASE PRINT
Please circle: Mr.   Mrs.   Miss   Rev.

Name _____

Address _____

City _____   State _____   Zip _____

Phone (___) _____

Email _____

☐ I give Gospel for Asia permission to send me emails (i.e. field stories, urgent prayer requests, etc.).
☐ I give Gospel for Asia permission to send me text messages (i.e. urgent updates, etc.).
Privacy Policy: Gospel for Asia will not sell, lease or trade your personal information.

HB52-RB9C

GOSPEL FOR ASIA'S
BRIDGE OF HOPE
CHILDREN'S MINISTRY

ECFA

BEST

Enhancing Trust

I want to make a DIFFERENCE!

I want more children to have the hope of a better future—now and for eternity.

> You will receive a photo and biography of each Bridge of Hope child you sponsor.

> Gospel for Asia sends 100% of your Bridge of Hope support to the mission field. Nothing is taken out for administrative expenses. All donations are tax deductible as allowed by law.

Your stamp on this card is like an
additional donation!—Bro. K.P.

BUSINESS REPLY MAIL
FIRST-CLASS MAIL · PERMIT NO 1 · WILLS POINT TX

POSTAGE WILL BE PAID BY ADDRESSEE

GOSPEL FOR ASIA
1116 ST THOMAS WAY
WILLS POINT TX 75169-9911

fold before tearing

Sponsor a child, get news
from the mission field
and order other
GFA materials
online at

WWW.GFA.ORG

How do you choose which children to enroll in GFA Bridge of Hope?

One of the hardest things to witness is the large number of little boys and girls looking into our GFA Bridge of Hope centers wanting to be involved, but unable to join.

Selection is primarily based on the needs of the children and on the prayers of our staff members. The hardest part is turning down child after child and seeing them suffer without firsthand contact with the love of the Lord. Honestly, there are so many children out there who need our help. One of the biggest requests from our leaders on the mission field is, "Can we please open up more centers? There are so many children here who need our help."

As we have the resources, we proceed with opening more centers. But there are so many times I have to tell our leaders "not yet." Selection is a painful process, but the staff at the centers, in partnership with the pastors of the local churches, pray through the needs of the children and the community. They reach out to all they can.

What is a typical day like for a GFA Bridge of Hope child?

Monday through Friday, the children are educated in all the subjects relevant to their age group. We have a holistic approach. Instead of focusing entirely on increasing the knowledge of the children or simply improving their physical health, GFA Bridge of Hope invests in their overall development.

In the afternoon, the teachers and staff help our students individually with the subjects they were taught in the morning. There are opportunities for them to practice their mathematics, science and arts. Reading and writing are two major skills every child learns at a GFA Bridge of Hope center. These are fundamental to liberating them from the cycle of poverty they have been trapped in all of their lives.

Through guidance from the staff, these children start to excel in their studies. Each one performs better once they receive this personal love and assistance from the staff.

Students also develop social skills in this safe atmosphere as they watch leaders set a good example. They play games and sports to help them learn teamwork, respect, good manners and how to cooperate with one another. They discover that they are all children of the Lord, equally loved and cared for.

Every day, GFA Bridge of Hope children have the opportunity to hear about the Lord. There are times of singing action songs, reciting memory verses and learning Bible stories such as when David slew Goliath, when Moses led the people of Israel across the Red Sea or when God created Adam and Eve.

Then every week, they learn something about how to take care of their bodies. These are simple practices such as brushing their hair and trimming their nails. Also provided for them every day is a nutritious meal, something many of the children will not have waiting for them at home. Vitamins are distributed, as they are needed, to keep the children healthy and to prevent problems such as blindness caused by a vitamin A deficiency. New school supplies and personal care items are handed out periodically, along with uniforms and books.

Each day is a special day for the children enrolled in GFA Bridge of Hope. For most of them, this is the only place they will ever get the chance to just be a kid!

The goal of GFA Bridge of Hope is to assist children to grow into godly individuals who will make a positive impact on their society. We want to give them the opportunity to become doctors, government officials, firemen, engineers, teachers, pastors, business leaders and godly parents. It is our hope that each of these children will become a responsible citizen, filled with the grace and love of the Lord, eager to spread His name throughout their communities in both word and deed.

HOW DOES A GFA BRIDGE OF HOPE CENTER CHANGE A COMMUNITY?

A GFA Bridge of Hope center transforms a community from within. Individually, the children act as beacons of hope for their families, friends and communities. Their behaviors are changed through GFA Bridge of Hope once they realize they have value in the eyes of the Lord. Soon they grow in newness of life. They stop stealing, cursing and running amok, instead becoming decent and respectful children.

We encourage them to tell others what they have learned. Time and time again, we have seen how the words of these little ones affect the hearts of their parents and turn them to the Lord. The light in children shines forth quite brilliantly!

As a whole, each GFA Bridge of Hope center acts as a nexus for community activity. The children put on an annual Christmas program. They invite people to celebrate Children's day, Parent's day and other holidays. Their obvious joy and enthusiasm draw many townsfolk to the center to observe what is going on. Almost always there are people whose lives are eternally changed by what they see and hear.

There are special community health sessions, teaching about such matters as brushing teeth and preventing AIDS. Counseling is available, and the staff visits the homes to minister to and pray for parents.

There are literacy classes and vocational training where people can learn such skills as how to sew or fish.

A GFA Bridge of Hope center brings hope to the entire community. When the townspeople see the staff unconditionally loving the children, they want to know more. This is when they experience the incredible care that Jesus has for older generations as well. The result is that they just naturally want to know about this God who leads people forward and gives them such value.

WHAT MAKES GFA BRIDGE OF HOPE UNIQUE?

The children at GFA Bridge of Hope centers have the opportunity to be transformed, not only because of the physical means of food, clothing and a practical education, including the amazing blessing of being able to read the written word, but also through the power of Jesus Christ. Although we are committed to alleviating the pains of this present world through physical aid and education, we are even more concerned about the eternal fate of these precious children.

GFA Bridge of Hope is a natural extension of our mission to reach the unreached with the love of Christ. Literally tens of thousands of people experience the love of God through our GFA Bridge of Hope ministry alone, but this is just the initial fruit of a much greater harvest. It is our hope that each child will spread this divine love they receive to all those around them. So one becomes five, which becomes twenty, then a hundred and even a thousand. These numbers will be even higher when we have more centers.

There are still millions of children who are eagerly waiting. And it's our heart's desire to reach them, not only with the promise that education brings, but also with the transforming power of the love of Christ.

HOW DOES US$35/MONTH PROVIDE FOR A CHILD ENROLLED IN GFA BRIDGE OF HOPE?

The support that is given provides a child with an education and personal help with their studies; it also gives them school supplies like books and backpacks and a clean and sturdy uniform to wear. Children receive practical items like towels and toothpaste. Each day they are served a nutritious meal, and every year there is a medical checkup with a trained doctor. Most important, this child will receive the personal care of the Living God, as manifested through the prayers and presence of GFA Bridge of Hope staff.

There is much more to educating children than simply filling their heads with facts and figures. Our staff knows how important it is that the students understand they are not doomed to the same fate as their parents and grandparents, but that they have the potential to literally change the world in which they live.

HOW DOES THE SPONSORSHIP MONEY REACH THE CHILDREN?

Gospel for Asia is firmly committed to good stewardship of the funds entrusted to us. GFA sends 100 percent of child sponsorship donations directly to the GFA Bridge of Hope school programs on the field without deducting anything for administrative costs.

When a donation is sent to GFA, we forward the monies to the field office in the nation where that child lives. The funds are then exchanged for local currency and sent to the leaders who oversee the center in which that child is enrolled.

As a sponsor of a GFA Bridge of Hope child, what should I expect?

As a sponsor, you will have the incredible blessing of being able to pray for a specific child on the other side of the world. And though you may never meet, we believe the impact your prayers will have on this child and his or her family will truly change their lives. You will also have the opportunity to write to your child and receive letters in return. On average, a child will write two letters per year.

Your role is a vital one. As your child's sponsor, you give donations that provide for a valuable education and lay the foundation for a future of promise. Your ongoing prayers for your sponsored child are another investment that has the potential to bear eternal rewards—not only in one child's heart but also in their family and community. It is entirely possible that thousands of people will be affected.

Your child will be praying for you as well, because you will become special to him or her and to their family. Many parents have a hard time fully understanding why a stranger on the other side of the world would want to send their child to school, feed them and buy them clothes. Your giving will help open their hearts to the Word of God.

You may never know the full effect of your support, because when you make a difference in the life of a child, your impact never really ends.

Your family can be changed through sponsorship too. Many sponsors find it an excellent way to bond as a family.

You will receive in the mail a photo and information packet about your child, which will help you know how to pray for him or her. Remember, you will be your child's only supporter.

DO I NEED TO COMMIT TO SPONSORING FOR A CERTAIN LENGTH OF TIME?

Although we give sponsors the opportunity to support children throughout their entire education, no time commitment is required.

We are convinced of the Lord's sovereignty, deep love and abundant provision for all these children. Depending on individual situations, some supporters may desire to assist their sponsored child for the entire length of his or her education, while others choose to do so for only a year or two. We understand that your circumstances could change. You may discontinue your sponsorship at any time, and we will find another sponsor to help the children you supported.

HOW CAN I GET TO KNOW MY SPONSORED CHILD BETTER?

There are several ways to learn more about your child, the country they live in and the GFA Bridge of Hope ministry.

1. Read the articles on our website, www.gfa.org/slumdog, in our emails and in our literature that highlight news about GFA Bridge of Hope programs across Asia. These articles spotlight children whose lives, families and communities have been changed through their encounters with God and His love.

2. We highly recommend the book *Operation World* by Jason Mandryk as a helpful resource for understanding both the culture and prayer needs of the nation in which your sponsored child lives. More information is available at www.operationworld.org.

3. You will receive at least two letters per year from your sponsored child. Here are several examples of letters from children:

Dear Rachael Smith,
    Hello.
    Hello, Rachael, how are you? I am fine. I am very happy to getting your letter. Thank you very-very much for all you have send me. Thank you for the beautiful pictures you send me. How lovely these are, God will bless. I agree with you that you and me are friends. Now you are my best friend. I am very thankful to God so that He will met you to me. I am very lucky that you are my friend. Thank you for your wish of Birthday. I enjoyed my birthday. Again I want to thank you for all you have send me. God will help you. God is great.
    Thanking you, with prayers,
    Yours lovingly,
    Danvir (12)

Dear Nathan and Olivia White,
    Hello.
    Praise the Lord. How are you? I hope you will be fine. I am fine and my family is doing well. I am going school for getting good education. My teachers are very kind and always helps us. I learned many good things in school. Thank you for writing me letter. I am always waiting for your letter. Always you inspired me for God's greatness. I love you people because you believe in God. I also believe in God very much. God will be help for you. Thanking you please keep pray for me.
    Thanking you with prayers,
    Yours lovingly,
    Lomash (11)

Dear Miss Kiersten Oliver,

How are you? Warmest greetings to you in the name of Jesus. By the grace of God, I am safe. Hoping you are also same.

By the love you are showing, I am able to go to school regularly and study well. We are benefited in many ways by the Bridge of Hope, such as getting Education, learning, Bible stories and verses, participating in weekly contest quiz games etc. I am also attending to the Sunday school.

These two months we got away-rains, all the rivers over flowing. The lower places are flooded. Many people lost their lives. Some lost their homes. Many are suffering with different problems. Please pray for our state.

In the project center we are taught how to pray in the morning, evening and at the time of study, meals etc. We are getting healthy food in the project. I thank God a lot. Please pray for me. I do pray for you.

Yours lovingly,

Rahdak (11)

Corresponding with your sponsored child not only strengthens your relationship, but also will be a great encouragement to everyone involved. You can personally write to your child using the special stationery and envelopes GFA provides. Your initial letter-writing material will be included in your sponsorship packet.

What is the ministry of Gospel for Asia?

Gospel for Asia is a nonprofit organization born out of an intense desire to reach people who have never before heard the name of Jesus. More than 30 years ago, God specifically called us to invest our lives to reach the most unreached of South Asia.

Today, we have several thousand national missionaries who minister in some of the most remote places on the face of this earth. You will find GFA-supported workers in the slums of major cities and among leper colonies. Our people also travel to the most remote desert places like Rajasthan and to the cold, isolated villages in the high reaches of the Himalayas. Our mission is to bring these people the hope found in Christ, and we do this through both physical assistance and a dedication to prayer and the preaching of the Gospel.

We act as Christ's witnesses, especially focused among the most unreached in Asia. We work by all means to see that not only are people's lives transformed, but also that these people become disciples of the Lord.

GFA Bridge of Hope is a natural extension of this desire to reach the unreached. People are usually more receptive to the Gospel after they witness our efforts to help their children and observe the great love and joy with which our staff works. Once they see their children blossom, parents want to learn more about who we are and why we are helping them. This acts as an open door to share the message of Christ's love.

WHAT PERCENTAGE OF DONATIONS DO YOU KEEP TO PAY FOR YOUR ADMINISTRATIVE COSTS?

None. Since Gospel for Asia's inception more than 30 years ago, we have been dedicated to giving 100 percent of the gifts given for the field to the field. We take nothing out for overhead expenses. Our buildings, administrative costs, advertising money and any other expenses that arise are covered by a separate fund.

GFA is a charter member of the Evangelical Council for Financial Accountability (ECFA). We fully support the purposes and goals of the ECFA and display its seal to reflect compliance with its membership standards.

BELIEVE IT OR NOT

THE 4/14 WINDOW are children between the ages of 4 and 14. These are the critical years when a child's character and worldview are molded.[1]

➤ 1.2 billion children worldwide are in the 4/14 Window.[2]

  ➤ More than 300 million children—one-fourth of the entire 4/14 Window—live in the South Asian countries of India, Bangladesh, Myanmar, Nepal and Sri Lanka.[3]

    ➤ If these South Asian children formed their own nation, its population would be as large as the United States.

CHILD LABOR standards have been established by the United Nations to protect children from exploitation in the workplace.

➤ 150 million of the 4/14 Window are child laborers, employed in violation of these standards.[4]

  ➤ 60 percent of these child laborers are 11 years or younger.[5]

    ➤ More than 50 million children are in "hazardous work" involving long hours; physical, psychological or sexual abuse; or dangerous equipment, confined spaces or toxic environments.[6]

➤ UNICEF estimates India's child labor population to be 30 million.[7] Other reliable sources believe the number is closer to 50 million.[8]

HUMAN TRAFFICKING is one of the fastest-growing criminal enterprises in the world today, soon to surpass the drug trade.

➤ 2.5 million people around the world are in forced labor at any given time as a result of trafficking.[9]

➤ More than half of trafficking victims are from Asia and the Pacific.[10]

➤ Every year, an estimated 1.2 million children become victims of trafficking.[11]

- Nepali women and girls, some as young as 9 years old, are sold into India's red-light district—10,000 to 15,000 per year.[12]

- Sri Lanka is touted as a pedophile's paradise, with up to 40,000 child prostitutes—mostly boys— trafficked to serve tourists.[13]

- 300,000 children worldwide are currently trafficked as child soldiers.[14]

INDIA'S POPULATION of 1.2 billion is made up of a few "haves" and a great many "have-nots."

➤ The "Brahmins"—about 5 percent of the population— dominate the country politically, socially and economically.[15]

- At the opposite extreme of Indian society are the Dalits—250 million people—who are treated like slaves and considered less valuable than animals.[16]
  - Another 500 million people in India suffer from need and abuse as members of "Other Backward Castes."[17]
    - Dalits and OBCs together make up more than 60 percent of India's population; this is as many people as live in all of Europe.

IMPROVED SANITATION FACILITIES are available for only about one out of three people in India.[18]

- That means that up to 800 million people use public or private latrines that must be cleaned by "manual scavengers."
  - This is the job of more than a million Dalits in India.[19]

Notes

TERMS AND CONCEPTS

1. "Brahmins in India," *Outlook India* (http://www. outlookindia.com/article.aspx?234783). (Accessed March 22, 2011).

INTRODUCTION

1. *Slumdog Millionaire*. DVD. Directed by Danny Boyle. 2009. Christian Colson.

2. Jason Mandryk, *Operation World: 7th edition* (Colorado Springs, CO: Biblica, 2010), p. 410.

3. Luis Bush, "The 4-14 Window – 'The Core of the Core,'" *4-14 Window Global Initiative* (http://4to14window. com/4-14-window-core-core). (Accessed March 21, 2011).

4. Mandryk, *Operation World*, p. 432.

CHAPTER 1: STOLEN CHILDHOOD

1. Daniel Berrigan, "Communion," *inward/outward: A Project of the Church of the Saviour* (http://www.inwardoutward. org/author/daniel-berrigan). (Accessed March 21, 2011).

2. UNICEF, *The State of the World's Children: 2005* (http://www.unicef.org/sowc05/english/sowc05_chapters.pdf). (Accessed March 24, 2011).

3. Mandryk, *Operation World,* p. 410.

4. Ibid., p. 410.

5. Ibid., p. 445.

6. Chris Morris, "Diet of Mud and Despair in Indian Village," *BBC News* (http://news.bbc.co.uk/2/hi/8682558.stm). (Accessed March 21, 2011).

7. Yacouba Diallo et al., *Global Child Labour Developments: Measuring Trends from 2004 to 2008* (Geneva: International Labour Office, 2010), p. 10.

8. UNICEF, *The State of the World's Children: Special Edition* (New York, NY: UNICEF, 2009), p. 24.

9. Megha Bahree, "Child Labor," *Forbes.com* (http://www.forbes.com/forbes/2008/0225/072.html). (Accessed March 21, 2011).

10. Ibid.

11. Joseph D'souza, *Dalit Freedom: Now and Forever* (Centennial, CO: Dalit Freedom Network, 2004), p. 42.

12. Mandryk, *Operation World,* p. 410.

13. "Child Labour," *Aide Internationale pour l'enfance* (http://www.aipe-cci.org/en/child-labor/en-enfants-travail.html). (Accessed March 21, 2011).

CHAPTER 2: ONCE A SLUMDOG, ALWAYS A SLUMDOG

1. Mother Teresa, *Where There Is Love, There Is God: A Path to Closer Union with God and Greater Love* (New York, NY: Doubleday Religion, 2010), p. 82.

2. "Advocating the Rights of the Marginalised for Justice and Equality," *Dalit Solidarity* (http://www.dalitsolidarity.org/). (Accessed March 21, 2011).

3.   "Dalits fined for daring to drink water from tap," *Dalit Freedom Network* (http://www.dalitnetwork.org/go?/dfn/news/2010/10/). (Accessed March 21, 2011).

4.   K.P. Yohannan, "I Am Nobody."

5.   K.P. Yohannan, "Vendor of Sticks."

6.   "Dalit beaten to death in Uttar Pradesh," *Thaindian News* (http://www.thaindian.com/newsportal/uncategorized/dalit-beaten-to-death-in-uttar-pradesh_100205461.html). (Accessed March 21, 2011).

7.   Mandryk, *Operation World,* p. 408.

8.   D'souza, *Dalit Freedom,* p. 37.

9.   National Sample Survey Organization, Ministry of Statistics and Programme Implementation, Government of India, *Employment and Unemployment Situation Among Social Groups in India 2004–05: NSS 61st Round (July 2004–June 2005),* Report No. 516, October 2006, pp. 21–22.

10. Mandryk, *Operation World,* p. 410.

Chapter 3: Open Your Eyes

1.   John Cook, comp., *The Book of Positive Quotations,* 2nd ed., ed.Steve Deger and Leslie Ann Gibson (Minneapolis, MN: Fairview Press), p. 112.

Chapter 4: Winds of Change

1.   Martin Luther King Jr. "I've Been to the Mountain Top" (speech, Mason Temple, Memphis, TN, April 3, 1968).

2.   K.P. Yohannan, *Revolution in World Missions* (Carrollton, TX: GFA Books, 2004), p. 29.

3.   "Discrimination: Briefing on Dalit and the Caste System," *Child Rights Information Network* (http://www.crin.org/resources/infoDetail.asp?ID=20802&flag=report). (Accessed March 21, 2011).

4.   Alex Perry, "Bombay's Boom," *TIME,* June 26, 2006.

5. "Poor mothers set up 'kid bazaar,' " *The Telegraph* (http://www.telegraphindia.com/1110108/jsp/siliguri/story_13407595.jsp). (Accessed March 21, 2011).

Chapter 5: It Is Happening

1. William Shakespeare, *The Merchant of Venice* (New York, NY: Washington Square Press, 1992).

2. "2004: Thousands die in Asian tsunami," *BBC* (http://news.bbc.co.uk/onthisday/hi/dates/stories/december/26/newsid_4631000/4631713.stm). (Accessed March 21, 2011).

Chapter 6: What Now?

1. James R. Lowell, *The Writings of James Russell Lowell in Prose and Poetry* (James Russell Lowell, 1870), p. 243.

2. Mandryk, *Operation World,* p. 410.

3. UNICEF, *The State of the World's Children: Special Edition,* p. 25.

4. Steven Curtis Chapman, "What Now," Copyright © September 21, 2004, Sparrow Records (adm. Worldwide by EMI CMG Publishing). All rights reserved.

5. E.M. Bounds, *Power Through Prayer* (Radford, VA: Wilder Publications, 2008), p. 15.

Chapter 7: Make Your Life Count

1. Linda Picone, *The Daily Book of Positive Quotations* (Minneapolis, MN: Fairview Press, 2008), p. 163.

2. C.S. Lewis, *The Screwtape Letters* (New York, NY: Macmillan, 1982), p. 61. (paraphrased)

3. 2007. *George Burns–I Wish I Was Eighteen Again* [Video], Retrieved February 3, 2011, from http://www.youtube.com/watch?v=F3c-WBn5cCg. (Accessed March 21, 2011).

4. Amy Carmichael, *Things as They Are: Mission Work in Southern India* (Princeton, NJ: Princeton University, 1906), p. 158.

APPENDIX II: BELIEVE IT OR NOT

1. The United Nations statistics cited in this book cover the 10-year age range from 5 to 14.

2. Diallo et al., *Global Child Labour Developments: Measuring Trends from 2004 to 2008,* p. 10.

3. Estimated by combining statistics on the "Under 15" population from *2010 World Population Data Sheet* (Washington, D.C.: Population Reference Bureau, 2010), pp. 6–9 with statistics on the "Under 5" population from *The State of the World's Children, Special Edition: Statistical Tables* (New York: UNICEF, 2009), pp. 28–31.

4. Diallo et al., *Global Child Labour Developments: Measuring Trends from 2004 to 2008,* p. 10.

5. Ibid., p. 10.

6. Ibid., p. 10.

7. UNICEF, *The State of the World's Children, Special Edition: Statistical Tables,* p. 41.

8. Mandryk, *Operation World,* p. 410.

9. United Nations Office on Drugs and Crime, *Human Trafficking FAQs* (http://www.unodc.org/unodc/en/human-trafficking/faqs.html). (Accessed March 21, 2011).

10. United Nations Global Initiative to Fight Human Trafficking, *Human Trafficking: The Facts* (http://www.unglobalcompact.org/docs/issues_doc/labour/Forced_labour/HUMAN_TRAFFICKING_-_THE_FACTS_-_final.pdf). (Accessed March 21, 2011).

11. UNICEF, *Child Protection Information Sheet: Trafficking* (http://www.unicef.org/protection/files/trafficking.pdf). (Accessed March 21, 2011).

12. U.S. Department of State, *Trafficking in Persons Report 2009,* p. 217 (http://www.state.gov/documents/organization/123357.pdf). (Accessed March 21, 2011).

13. International Labour Organization, *Anti-Child Trafficking Legislation in Asia: A Six-Country Review,* 2006, p. 70 (http://www.ilo.org/wcmsp5/groups/public/---asia/---ro-bangkok/documents/publication/wcms_bk_pb_76_en.pdf). (Accessed March 21, 2011).

14. UNICEF, *Children in Conflict and Emergencies* (http://www.unicef.org/protection/index_armedconflict.html). (Accessed March 21, 2011).

15. Sudha Ramachandran, "Caste Politics Come Full Circle," *Asia Times Online,* March 26, 2009 (http://www.atimes.com/atimes/South_Asia/KC26Df01.html). (Accessed March 21, 2011).

16. National Sample Survey Organization, *Employment and Unemployment Situation Among Social Groups in India 2004–05: NSS 61st Round,* pp. 21–22.

17. Ibid., pp. 21–22.

18. *2010 World Population Data Sheet,* p. 16. An improved sanitation facility is one that hygienically separates sewage from human contact.

19. CHR&GJ and Human Rights Watch, *On the Margins of Profit: Rights at Risk in the Global Economy,* vol. 20, no. 3(G), February 2008, p. 31 (http://www.hrw.org/sites/default/files/reports/bhr0208_1.pdf). (Accessed March 21, 2011).

About Gospel for Asia

God specifically called us to invest our lives to reach the most unreached in Asia through training and sending out national missionaries. Today, thousands of GFA-supported workers serve fulltime to bring the Gospel to those still waiting to hear.

To train national missionaries and share the love of Christ throughout Asia, Gospel for Asia

- supports Bible colleges
- airs radio broadcasts
- distributes Gospel literature
- offers education and hope to Asia's poorest children
- cares for leprosy patients and widows
- digs wells to provide pure water
- provides relief after natural disasters

Visit **www.gfa.org** to learn more about these and other ministries of Gospel for Asia and to discover how you can get involved. While there, be sure to order your free copy of K.P. Yohannan's best-selling book *Revolution in World Missions*.

Gospel for Asia Offices

AUSTRALIA P.O. Box 3587, Toowoomba QLD 4350
Freephone: 1300 889 339   Email: infoaust@gfa.org

CANADA 245 King Street E, Stoney Creek, ON L8G 1L9
Toll free: 1-888-WIN-ASIA   Email: info@gfa.ca

FINLAND PL 63, FI-65101, Vaasa
Phone: 050 036 9699   Email: infofi@gfa.org

GERMANY Postfach 13 60, 79603 Rheinfelden (Baden)
Phone: 07623 79 74 77   Email: infogermany@gfa.org

KOREA Seok-Am Blg 5th floor, 6-9 Tereran-ro 25 gil, Yeoksam-dong,
Gangnam-gu, Seoul 135-080
Toll free: (080) 801-0191   Email: infokorea@gfa.org.kr

NEW ZEALAND PO Box 302580, North Harbour 0751
Toll free: 0508-918-918   Email: infonz@gfa.org

SOUTH AFRICA P.O. Box 28880, Sunridge Park, Port Elizabeth 6008
Phone: 041 360-0198   Email: infoza@gfa.org

UNITED KINGDOM PO Box 316, Manchester M22 2DJ
Phone: 0161 946 9484   Email: infouk@gfa.org

UNITED STATES 1116 St. Thomas Way, Wills Point, TX 75169
Toll free: 1-800-WIN-ASIA   Email: info@gfa.org

"O God,
let just one of my boys preach."

A mother's prayer continues to change the world today.

Find out how God answered that prayer and redeemed millions of lives in Asia through the missions movement started by K.P. Yohannan. And discover how his story can change your life, too.

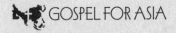 GOSPEL FOR ASIA

OTHER MATERIALS
FROM GOSPEL FOR ASIA

NO LONGER A SLUMDOG

You've read it; now share it with friends and family members!

Special pricing is available on bulk orders. Please contact the GFA office near you for details.

TOUCHING GODLINESS

NEW EDITION WITH STUDY GUIDE. It is not enough to be on the sidelines and watch others enter into godliness. It is *for you and me.* Writing with fatherly concern, K.P. Yohannan challenges us to follow Christ down the path of surrender and submission and, in the end, find God's promised "life abundant."

DESTINED TO SOAR

Does it feel like life is closing in on you? K.P. Yohannan shows you the way to rise above the weight of this world and keep your true purpose in clear view. Relevant and incredibly practical, his hope-filled approach to critical issues frees you to be all for Jesus.

Order online at *www.gfa.org/store*
Or contact the GFA office near you.
National offices are listed on page 166.

LIVING IN THE LIGHT OF ETERNITY

This book will challenge you to look beyond temporary concerns of life to what will last forever. You will gain a solid basis for genuine spiritual growth as you learn to organize your priorities in the light of eternity.

LET ME WALK WITH YOU

Are you feeling alone or overwhelmed in your journey with the Lord Jesus? In this volume of letters, originally addressed to women serving on the challenging mission fields of South Asia, Gisela Yohannan shares precious lessons from her own life and insights from God's Word that will fill your heart with faith and strength, no matter where you are in your walk with Jesus. By His grace, you *will* make it!

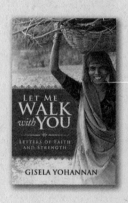

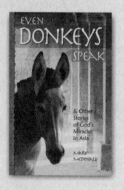

EVEN DONKEYS SPEAK

This children's book is a collection of stories taken straight from the mission fields of South Asia. As you read these exciting tales of God at work, you and your youngsters will feel as if you are right there with these believers, following the Lord amid the steaming jungles and cold mountain villages of Asia. It's great reading, no matter your age.

TOUCH OF LOVE

You will be inspired as K.P. Yohannan takes you around the world to see the "Untouchable" children of Asia through Jesus' eyes. His message will help you better understand the heart of Christ, who calls these children His own—and give you a chance to reach them with His eternal love.

TO LIVE IS CHRIST!

Feel the passion of K.P. Yohannan as he describes the life-giving power of total commitment to Christ in this 55-minute DVD. Be amazed by stories of missionaries who risk their lives to preach the Gospel. Weep with him as he recalls his mother's years of sacrifice that changed lives for eternity. Many people search in vain for the path that leads to the abundant life that Jesus promised. K.P., through the Word of God, uncovers that path in this inspiring and challenging message.

VEIL OF TEARS (DVD)

Take an unforgettable journey to South Asia, where women for centuries have been culturally oppressed and abused simply because they were born female. Today, through Gospel for Asia, the Church is reaching out to these precious women, bringing hope and restoring dignity to their shattered lives. Enter into the tragedies and triumphs of the women you'll meet in this award-winning documentary film, narrated by Natalie Grant.

Order online at *www.gfa.org/store*
Or contact the GFA office near you.
National offices are listed on page 166.

FREE EMAIL UPDATES
Sign up today at gfa.org/email

Hear from today's heroes of the mission field.

Have their stories and prayer requests sent straight to your inbox.

- **Fuel your prayer life with compelling news and photos from the mission field.**

- **Stay informed with links to important video and audio clips.**

- **Learn about the latest opportunities to reach the lost world.**

GFA sends updates every week. You may cancel your free subscription at any time. We will not sell or release your email address for any reason.

Travel to the mission field—
for a few hours

Even though you don't live with the millions of people in South Asia or experience their unique cultures and struggles, you can intercede for them!

By joining in **Gospel for Asia's live-streaming prayer meetings**, you can step inside their world through stories, photos and videos. You might even change, too. Here's what other people said about the prayer meetings:

"I don't think I ever come away with a dry eye from these prayer meetings. It is so encouraging to me to see the Lord working so mightily in so many ways in the world."
—Sheri

"It is so good and helpful to hear of the needs and to sense God's Spirit at work. It helps me to pray more earnestly and to be a part of what God is doing in your ministry."
—Timothy

"Praise Jesus! I love having a team to pray with."
—Mia

Pray with us!
Go to **www.gfa.org/pray** for schedules and to participate in the streamed prayer meetings.